'This important myth-busting bo[ok offers socio]logical explanations and confro[nts street life at] their religious root. Moses effecti[vely frames a worldview] and-life view with the heart and [mind of] both the evangelist and prophet, combining careful biblical thinking with his own story of deliverance from the ways of the streets. *The Streets vs The Kingdom* is a compelling resource for urban youth exposed to violence, young offenders, parents, teachers, social workers, police officers, and church leaders who need to better understand a subculture that desperately needs Christ. Equip yourself with this challenging new work.'

—REV DR. JOSEPH BOOT, FOUNDER, EZRA INSTITUTE FOR CONTEMPORARY CHRISTIANITY; AUTHOR, 'THE MISSION OF GOD'

'When Moses approached me to read through his manuscript I felt an overwhelming sense of inadequacy. My formative years were spent in a small town in Devon, so my exposure to the streets only came when I moved to London. However, I have gone on to witness firsthand the devastating effect the streets can have on an individual's life. Moses has taken biblical truths and applied them to almost every aspect of the street mindset and mentality. He interweaves his personal testimony and experience together with his knowledge of the word of God, to bring hope to those who feel that they can never break out or break free from the streets. This book is a must read, and I highly recommend it.'

—LEIGHTON AINSWORTH, PASTOR, POTTER'S HOUSE SOUTH LONDON; AUTHOR, 'BE ONE, MAKE ONE: REAL DISCIPLESHIP'

'*The Streets vs The Kingdom* is an excellent book that highlights the need for the light of Jesus to break into the darkness of street culture amongst young people, especially young men. Using a blend of personal stories, real life examples and powerful insights, Moses draws out some of the root causes and issues that young people are facing and shows us how the Gospel is the answer to them all. A book packed with Scripture and truth, yet written in a style and tone that is easy to engage with and understand. A must read for anyone who is passionate about young people!'

–JOE MACNAMARA, PASTOR, KING'S CHURCH LONDON

THE STREETS
vs
THE KINGDOM

THE STREETS
VS
THE KINGDOM

HOW GOD'S TRUTH SETS US FREE

MOSES NWANJI

SAFEHAVENPRINTS.COM

THE STREETS VS THE KINGDOM

Copyright © 2025 by Moses Nwanji

ISBN 978-1-0685516-0-4 (Paperback)
ISBN 978-1-0685516-1-1 (eBook)

The moral right of the author under the Copyright, Designs and Patents Act 1988 has been asserted.

All rights reserved. No part of this publication may be reproduced, stored in a retrieval system or transmitted in any form or by any means—for example, electronic, photocopy, recording—without the prior written permission of the publisher. The only exception is brief quotations in printed reviews.

Unless otherwise indicated, all scriptures are taken from the Holy Bible, New International Version® Anglicised, UK version NIVUK® Copyright © 1979, 1984, 2011 by Biblica, Inc.® Used by permission. All rights reserved worldwide.

All scripture quotations marked NKJV are from the New King James Version®. Copyright © 1982 by Thomas Nelson, Inc. Used by permission. All rights reserved.

All scripture quotations marked ESV are from The ESV® Bible (The Holy Bible, English Standard Version®), copyright © 2001 by Crossway, a publishing ministry of Good News Publishers. Used by permission. All rights reserved.

Unless otherwise indicated, all the names of characters in this book are fictitious. Any resemblance to actual persons, living or dead is purely coincidental.

Book designed by Mark Karis

Published in London, United Kingdom, by Safehaven Prints.

'So if the Son sets you free, you will be free indeed.'

JOHN 8:36

CONTENTS

Acknowledgements xi
Foreword xiii

   Introduction 1
1 Money over Everything vs. Seek First the Kingdom—Part 1 7
2 Money over Everything vs. Seek First the Kingdom—Part 2 21
3 Violence is the Way vs. Seek Peace 33
4 No Snitching vs. Expose the Works of Darkness 47
5 Women for My Pleasure vs. Women, God's Image Bearers 61
6 Make It out the Hood vs. Evil Leads to Destruction 75
7 The 'Real' Man vs. The True Man—Part 1 87
8 The 'Real' Man vs. The True Man—Part 2 97
   Conclusion 115

Prayer 122
Street Terms 124
Bible Terms 126

ACKNOWLEDGEMENTS

WHERE DO I START? It's easy—right with Jesus Christ. He is the reason I've been able to put pen to paper. There would be no Moses, let alone any book, if He did not set me free from the streets. Moreover, this book wouldn't be, if He didn't put it on my heart to share how He did it. You are wonderful and I'm thankful for your patience over these years of writing, but most importantly when I was in darkness and an enemy of yours.

I can never forget my wife, Francesca, who has been a constant source of encouragement and motivation. You have always believed that I was made for more, and have done all you can to see that come to fruition. You, my dear, are amazing, and I'm forever thankful that we're on the same team.

My parents. You were so pivotal on this journey. God answered your prayers and tears to save me from my sin. Thank

ACKNOWLEDGEMENTS

you for your sacrifice and love, for without it, I would not be writing this.

To my three precious children, thank you for trusting me (and your mum) with your lives. I want this book to reveal exactly where Jesus saved Daddy from and ultimately how God sets us free to live for Him. God loves you!

FOREWORD

IF YOU'RE HOLDING 'THE STREETS VS THE KINGDOM', it's not by chance. Maybe you're already living that life, or maybe you're watching friends or family spiral into that world. Either way, you're here for a reason—and I want to tell you, with everything I've lived through, that there's hope.

I go by the name Reblah now, though some may remember me as Rebler. My old tag name came from the streets of South East London, where I was known not only for my gift of rap, but for the life I was living—deeply immersed in gang culture. Rap gave me status and influence, but it also gave me a false sense of power, dragging me into a world of armed robbery, drug dealing and fraud. I was on a path of destruction, one that almost landed me behind bars, like so many of the people I ran with. By God's grace, I escaped that fate. If you asked me back then, I would've told you there were only two ways out: death or prison.

But I'm living proof that there's another way—freedom through Jesus Christ. And that's what 'The Streets vs The Kingdom' is all about. I first met Moses, the author of this powerful book, through my wife. She spoke highly of him, how he encouraged her academically and made her aware of various opportunities during university. But Moses' story is much deeper than just his success in life. Like me, he was trapped on the streets, but today, he's a transformed man, set free by the power of God. This transformation is what qualifies Moses to speak to you through these pages.

If you've ever wondered whether there's more to life than the streets, 'The Streets vs The Kingdom' will give you the answer. Moses doesn't just talk about change—he's lived it. He's from the ends, faced the same struggles, and made the same mistakes. Yet here he stands, on the other side, telling you that freedom is possible. This book is for you if you're caught in that cycle or know someone who is. It's for the young person about to make a choice that could change their life forever.

Through personal stories and biblical truths, Moses lays out a clear guide for avoiding the traps of this lifestyle. The first two chapters hit especially hard, tackling the idol of money and how its led so many down the wrong path.

But the message goes deeper than just practical advice. It's about spiritual freedom. Jesus didn't just come to give us a better life—He came to give us a new heart.

> Ezekiel 36:26 says, *I will give you a new heart and put a new spirit in you; I will remove from you your heart of stone and give you a heart of flesh.*

FOREWORD

That's exactly what He did for me. The streets hardened me, but Jesus softened my heart and gave me a purpose beyond anything I could have imagined. Today, I'm an award-winning Gospel artist, a husband, and a father to three incredible children, all because Jesus intervened. Reblah means 'the one Yahweh is proud of', and now I live to make God proud.

So, as you read 'The Streets vs The Kingdom', my prayer is that you'll be open to what God wants to do in your life. He set Moses free. He set me free. And I know—if you're willing—He'll set you free, too. Now's the time to turn the page and discover what's possible when you give your life to Christ.

INTRODUCTION

WHEN THE CYCLE of gang-related violence so common in the UK today is reported, it's rare to hear terms like 'indoctrination' or 'worldview' to explain why this is happening. Indoctrination is simply the process of making someone accept your ideas and beliefs, while worldview is an understanding of the world from a specific standpoint. Both are related, and, in a moment, I'll share how they heavily contribute to the devastation we see on our streets.

You've probably heard other words trotted out such as 'government cuts', 'poverty', 'no opportunities', 'deprived areas' and many more, to describe why young people take to the *streets*[1], despite the high cost to life. Of course, these points are valid. Social and economic issues do contribute to this wide problem, and, in fact, these verses from the Bible make clear that a lack of basic necessities (and also an abundance, by the way) can be tempting. That's why the writer of this Proverb says:

> *Two things I ask of you, Lord;*
>   *do not refuse me before I die:*

---

1   The gang life and all that comes with it. *See Street Terms for more.*

Keep falsehood and lies far from me;
   give me neither poverty nor riches,
   but give me only my daily bread.
Otherwise, I may have too much and disown you
   and say, "Who is the Lord?"
Or I may become poor and steal,
   and so dishonour the name of my God. (Proverbs 30:7-9)

I do not disagree with that sentiment. It does make sense that an improvement in one's social setting (i.e. education, jobs, food) can help reduce the number of people ending up in the depths of gang culture. But it only plays a part in the overall picture, and how much is very debatable. I, for one, know from first-hand experience, that, if I had been presented with a job opportunity during my time on the streets, I would have passed on it because a job would have removed me from the spotlight of the guys, girls and money that were so readily available.

I propose there is something else at play here that causes young people to gravitate to the streets, that we commentators on this topic tend to miss. In other words, tackling the system of the streets is not as simple as just throwing money at the situation or showcasing alternative financial prospects, however important. I know you understand what I'm saying. In fact, personally, it was the 'attractiveness' of the street life that took me off track from training towards my original dreams of becoming a sprinter or a footballer. To put it simply, there was something more appealing on the streets, something much stronger within, something at my core that was pulling me towards the streets and all it had to offer, regardless of the positive opportunities that presented themselves elsewhere.

And I'm sure you know the same is still true today, even when the odds are stacked against you. Negative opportunities, such as jail time for crimes committed, haven't been able to largely keep away young men (and women) from the trappings of the streets. In fact, you and I know that time in jail has even contributed to the image. If you've been to jail, the view is that the time spent actually earns you more clout and sets you to gain even greater status in the eyes of those who play by the rules of the streets.

Someone reading this, with no knowledge of this culture, may think this is crazy. But you and I know this is the worldview of the streets—the indoctrination, the lens through which its followers frame the world around them. Additionally, you are probably aware that one would be foolish enough to believe that this way of thinking is only adopted by the so-called active gang member. Non-participants, such as parents, neighbours, YouTube/social media spectators, and other sympathisers—even legal professionals—can and do subscribe to this mindset.

That is why, when serious discussions are held about how to tackle this grave evil, I think it is a big mistake to overlook the all-encompassing worldview that runs through the veins of the individuals who embrace this culture of death. A culture of death is what I call it because of the evil it perpetuates, that may have stunted your life and the lives of others, their families and society at large (both victims and perpetrators).

But, more importantly, it's an even bigger mistake to completely disregard the heart of every individual involved, as most do in discussions around youth violence today. Understanding the nature of the human heart, its makeup and its desires is key. For too long the conversation has focused on the external pressures alone, almost assuming every individual is innocent, has a heart of gold, and is intent on doing good. It's as good as saying, 'Change the externals and all will be well.'

I have come to realise that, at the root of this issue, are individuals, not structures. That's not to say that structures have no impact on an individual, because they do. But it's an individual that ultimately sets up a drug line in the hope of making a fortune. It's an individual who desires to make a name for himself on the streets, despite coming from a stable family. It's an individual who violently forces a young boy to join his gang, so as to use him. And it's an individual that poses with a popular gang member in a video, knowing full well that he has many people who want him hurt.

It's no surprise then that the Bible makes this striking claim: *The heart is deceitful above all things, and desperately sick; who can understand it?* (Jeremiah 17:9 ESV)

This is a strong statement, and one that I'd encourage you not to shrug off without giving it a thought. The verse is basically saying that the human heart—that place where your moral, intellectual and emotional choices are made—is diseased to the point where it gladly sides with activities and lifestyles that lead to death over and above those that result in life. The biggest and most foundational cause of this is the rejection of the God of life. This is where the root of the problem lies, and I would invite you to look again at my proposition at the beginning of this introduction to convince you that the human heart, not the area you're from or your family background, is what is fundamentally sick!

However, there is hope. There is One who not only understands our condition, but desires and is able to heal our hearts. This is why, apart from analysing social issues, or understanding the system of the streets and those enslaved by it, we need to be confronted by an absolute counterpoint: God's truth. Truth not

INTRODUCTION

only exposes the falsehood of the streets and all its consequences, but is also powerful enough to free all those who are bound by this stronghold[2]. Truth can transform their hearts and desires, and thereby rescue their life from destruction, and set them on a path to fruitfulness.

What is this truth? It's the Good News of the Lord Jesus Christ as recorded in the Bible. Jesus, by His word and power is able to rescue you, not only from this sea of sickness, but from the ultimate disease—sin[3]—that leads to eternal death. He did this for me, and I want to use this opportunity in this book to communicate His Kingdom message of hope, restoration and grace to you.

So, in the following chapters, I'm going to highlight six major beliefs or myths that the streets have most likely already indoctrinated in you—and which you may already be living by—and show you their error. But more than that, I'm going to show you how contrasting and life-transforming God's truth is, when applied to each specific stronghold.

My hope is that you will clearly see the poison that you have been fed or may still be feasting on—whether introduced to you by an *older*[4], your own desires (which is true for all), a music video or your surroundings, that is, the streets. But, above that, I hope you encounter the love, freedom, forgiveness[5] and purpose that is offered to all who enter God's Kingdom, by faith in the life, death and resurrection of the Lord Jesus Christ.

---

2 A strongly entrenched belief (usually negative) that binds an individual to a certain lifestyle. *See Bible Terms for more.*

3 The breaking of God's law. *See Bible Terms for more.*

4 An older gang-member. *See Street Terms for more.*

5 Forgiveness in the Bible is more than just words. It must come from the heart. *See Bible Terms for more.*

MONEY OVER EVERYTHING VS. SEEK FIRST THE KINGDOM—PART 1

1

SO, LET'S GET INTO IT. Have you ever heard of a pyramid scheme before? I think I first heard of them once or twice when I was younger, probably in a film or a TV series. But it was only when I started working in finance that I became more familiar with what pyramid schemes actually are. So far in my life, I haven't been duped by any—financial ones that is—though I know quite a few people who have.

In this chapter, my hope is to steer you away from becoming a dupe of an even greater scheme. I can assure you that, if you took a moment to consider the basic foundations of a pyramid scheme and then took a glance at the streets, you would see quite clearly the similarities between the two. This is true especially when you ponder the heart-capturing, national-anthem-like, belief, motto and myth: money over everything!

IT'S A PYRAMID SCHEME!

Pyramid schemes come in different shapes and guises. Some even distance themselves from pyramid schemes by calling themselves 'multilevel marketing'; but the principle is still the same. While I don't plan to give you a thorough breakdown of their structure, there are some important features they possess that I want you to become familiar with. You can then see what makes them so attractive to onlookers—despite being a sham—and how the streets have used a similar tactic to lure people like you into its trap.

Very simply, operators of pyramid schemes make money by recruiting as many people as possible into their lower ranks (bottom of the pyramid), with the unrealistic promise of high returns. These returns come either through recruiting other people to the scheme and/or through selling an item that usually has no real value to the person buying it. Can you already see the foolishness of this? On top of that, each new recruit to the scheme has to pay a fee (which obviously makes its way to the top of the pyramid), with the hope that, as they recruit more people, they also will start to benefit from the fees those beneath them now have to pay! You can see why the pyramid, as a shape, has been chosen to describe them, because the higher up the ranks you go, the better off you are financially; the narrower it gets, the fewer that make it there.

Now I'm hoping you are starting to piece together how this relates to this viral slogan often heard on the streets, 'Money over everything!' But if not, if you are still scratching your head, then keep on reading.

You might be asking by now why would someone even join a pyramid scheme if, by their very nature, they only benefit the few who are at the top? That's a good question and I wish all who entered one would ask this question before joining. But to give you an answer, apart from every scheme having their unique 'selling point', the most obvious reason that countless people are hoodwinked into joining them is … drumroll please! … the allure and promise of quick riches. Say 'quick' one more time because that's where the emphasis needs to be.

It doesn't take a rocket scientist to imagine that those who start pyramid schemes know full well that many people—just like themselves—desire to make money by putting in the least amount of work that is humanly possible. Am I lying? For instance, let me confess, I was one of those who, when the cryptocurrency craze (Bitcoin and the rest) was becoming mainstream back in 2017, 'invested' (read gambled) money with no knowledge of what I was actually investing in or the risks involved. And I'm supposed to be the financial guy as well! It says a lot about the decisions one can make when allured by the so-called promise of quick riches. All I wanted was the price of the asset to go higher, as it had been doing before I got on the train. But let's just say it didn't continue as planned! I'm sure that even now you can recall similar experiences where you or someone you know pounced at quick returns, without considering what you were getting yourselves into. We'll get into that in a moment.

WHY DO WE LOVE THEM?

But why does this happen? Why do we easily get bamboozled into following the path to quick riches? Well, there are many secondary reasons (e.g. a lack of funds), but the primary reason is because, as the Bible—God's truth to us—states, as I referenced in the Introduction, the heart of every human being is deceitful (Jeremiah 17:9). It's broken and, yes, that includes your heart too. Check this! If not for the abundance of evidence from gardeners, science and our local shops, many of us would shamelessly demand that our fruits should quickly appear before us, without first putting in the work of preparing the soil, planting the seeds and the other necessary processes involved in producing good fruit. We want things quick!

That's how broken the structure of our hearts are. We'd rather reap where we have not sown but, worse still, we blindly entertain and welcome those who sell us this dream, although it is dressed in different clothing. This is what the founders of pyramid schemes are doing when they entice people into their web. And guess what? It's the very same thing that rap artist on YouTube, friend or older from the area is doing, when they promote or draw you into life on the streets. They appeal to your internal desire for riches, by saying all you need to do is, 'Get this money or stack your paper' or, as is more commonly trumpeted, 'Money over everything!'

How? You ask. How are my guys selling me a dream? How am I entering a pyramid scheme and a trap by screaming and living out this motto: money over everything? Well, in order to answer your series of questions, let me first ask you some questions and see where it takes us.

- ***Who*** *do the streets mainly promote this motto to?*

- ***What*** *are the streets promising you if you live by this motto?*

- ***How many*** *people actually achieve what is promised?*

- *In reality,* ***what is the result*** *of living by this motto?*

I'm sure you've already arrived at some sort of answer to these four questions, whether it's from personal experience on the streets or simple guesswork. But regardless, let's look at each one together.

WHO DO THE STREETS MAINLY PROMOTE THIS MOTTO TO?

To the young, to the broke and to greedy persons. That was me indeed! Well, young and greedy at least. And that may well be you, too. There's nothing inherently wrong in being young and/or broke. We've all been naive and broke at some point.

But the system of the streets, and those caught up in it use both to their advantage. Let's be honest; the streets aren't trying to draw in grown men in need of some extra change to 'Come and get this money'. Instead, it comes after the young and inexperienced. You're the ideal candidate for this pyramid scheme!

Folly is bound up in the heart of a child ... says Proverbs 22:15.

Don't be thrown off by that word 'child'. Although it seems to imply toddlers and maybe primary-school aged kids, without a good dose of godly wisdom, discipline and direction, that folly will still be present even in your teenage years. I'm not saying that adults can't make foolish decisions—because they do—but more often than not you hear people saying, 'I wish I didn't make that dumb decision when I was younger.'

And it's this that the operators of the streets pyramid scheme exploit when they lure you in to 'Get this money'! They're fully aware that you aren't going to consider or possibly even know the full extent of the decisions you're making now. Who in their mid-teens ever considered that, if they got caught doing bank fraud, it could shatter their chances of getting on the property ladder via a mortgage in just ten years time? Or their chances of travelling to Miami? Not me! And the average gang member who brings you in surely isn't going to include that in their disclaimer form when you sign up. Why? Because they know, that as a young person you're likely only going to make your choice based on maybe one question alone—'Am I going to get paid?' You have no thought of the obvious risks involved.

Please don't take this as an insult, because it's not meant to be. I was this young person, out on the streets of London, trying to live out this motto and make this money. I wish I had known this when I was younger. This is why I am writing this chapter. But I want this point to hit you like a ton of bricks so that you can see your ways and the streets more clearly. In the same way bicycles have training wheels for learners, you'll appreciate my warnings if you can admit your vulnerabilities as a young person. Just as the bicycle learner who's fallen down many times will appreciate the training wheels; my hope is that even now—not when you fall—you will appreciate the words you're reading right here.

But let's continue! I said that the streets promote this motto not only to the young and/or broke, but also to the person who's greedy. This is key, because there are young people who come from not-too-well-off homes who haven't fallen for the trap of the streets. On the other hand, there are many young people who have come from homes and families that have enough, and yet for reasons that have nothing to do with poverty, have found themselves in the depths of life on the streets. Maybe you can relate to one of these descriptions.

I can definitely relate to the second one. My family weren't broke. We had food on the table each day. I had clothes on my back. We went on holidays at a time when some of my friends didn't even own a passport! We weren't rich, but we definitely weren't broke. Yet, in my mid-teens I found myself 'feeling' broke because I didn't have Kickers on my feet, or the latest Air Force 1's or an Avirex jacket on my back. My examples may reveal the generation (the 2000s) and city I grew up in, but I'm sure you can replace them with more relevant items, which can make you feel deprived if you're without.

The point is, I wasn't less fortunate and, if you're living in the same condition as I was, you aren't either. Instead, you're just covetous! Put simply, that's a state in which your lack of contentment leads you to greedily desire what others have. While contentment is the state of being satisfied with your portion in life, regardless of what you have. In all honesty, most of us struggle with being satisfied. That's why we covet what others have and then make it out to seem like we're disadvantaged or hard done by, and need to grind until we possess them.

> Jesus put it like this: *Watch out! Be on your guard against all kinds of greed; life does not consist in an abundance of possessions* (Luke 12:15).

Nevertheless, you may say, 'I hear what you're saying, but my family and I are really broke.' If that's you, I not only hear you but I feel you. I remember speaking with a friend called Carl about our childhood, and he mentioned a time when he and some friends regretfully robbed a pizza delivery man. That wasn't the only sad part though. He went on to share that, while most of his friends did it just for a laugh, he did so because he had no food to eat indoors. While the majority scuffled jokingly to get a share of the pizza, this young man did so like his life depended on it.

Are you or any of your friends going through a similar experience? If so, I'm sorry, because this is what it means to be broke, to be poor. That doesn't justify the actions taken, but it sure does reveal why you may be willing and more easily tempted to go on the streets and make money—be it through selling drugs, robbery or fraud. But, as you can already see, the streets and this motto it pushes—money over everything—is hardly concerned with lifting you or your family out of poverty for the near future. For if it was, you would be advised on how to budget, save and invest the money you've made so that it could build up over a period of time and change your situation dramatically.

Instead, the streets encourage you to spend this money on purchasing the latest and most expensive clothes (I haven't even mentioned weapons yet), so that you can strut around before the majority of your peers who obviously lack the finances for Louis Vuitton loafers. Meanwhile, as your pride and self-esteem climbs, that older who brought you in smiles comfortably as he continues to be fed, while you put yourself and your family at even greater risk through the activities you have to engage in to make money.

As a young person you may not see all of this right away, or maybe you already have, given your experience. But with this first question answered, I'm hoping you are already starting to see exactly why you, not anyone else, are the ideal candidate for this pyramid scheme, in just the same way operators of traditional pyramid schemes go fishing for those craving quick riches. Watch out!

WHAT ARE THE STREETS PROMISING YOU IF YOU LIVE BY THIS MOTTO?

It's obvious, money, money, money, money… money! And the not so obvious … the intangibles like happiness, status and fulfilment. I'm sure you'd agree with me on this. In fact, more than that, the streets go even further and say that, by living by this motto—money over everything—you will have the opportunity to do and get anything that you want! It's the money plus the (intangible) things money can afford. It could be the ability to buy food after school without worrying about the price, purchasing the latest trainers, getting a weapon to protect you from your enemies or even moving your family out of the area. No matter how ambitious your dreams are, this pyramid scheme convinces you that it can supply all of that, provided you subscribe to its rules and follow the process.

In fact, the olders play the part of role models in this scheme. These are those who have gone before you, who were once in your position but have now made it. Traditional pyramid schemes follow the same order. Hardly will you come across an operator of a pyramid scheme who appears broke. No! They will ensure that they look smart and speak enthusiastically, so as to convince you that following the path they're on will land you in a similar, if not, better place than they. This is exactly the same with the olders in the area—they look the part! They have the flashy car (though no one has told you about car finance yet), while you are still riding the bus or your bike; they can afford champagne, while you are still struggling to afford that 59p KA can drink.

These guys appear like superstars, and all you have to do is follow their lead and soon you will arrive too. This is what you're promised, but how many actually attain this?

HOW MANY PEOPLE ACTUALLY ACHIEVE WHAT IS PROMISED?

I could rephrase this question another way: how many people actually make it out of the hood? We're going to look at this myth in another chapter, but for the purpose of this exercise, why don't you take a shot: how many? I'm sure your experience on the streets or knowledge of it has informed you pretty well of what the answer is. But to put an end to speculation, the answer is quite obvious: few and far between!

It's no surprise then why I've compared life on the streets, and particularly this myth of money over everything, to a pyramid scheme. Many participate, but only a few ever emerge 'winners'! However, there aren't any true winners—but you get the point. And it's unfortunate that we don't have official statistics to illustrate this. For all those who have been lured into seeking money through this pyramid scheme of the streets, the overwhelming majority have fallen short of what they hoped for. This shouldn't be hard to understand.

As I write, I can recall numerous olders who were ahead and higher up the pyramid than I was when I joined in my teens. Yet, decades later, not only had they not reached the top but, worse still, they slid into an even more severe position than where they started. Take, for example, Tyrell who I was quite fond of growing up. He was popular in my area, wore a nice chunky chain, and was clearly moving up the ranks in terms of monetary gain from the streets. Yet, as you read this book, Tyrell sits within the walls of a UK jail, with a release date far into the future. I don't write this to bring shame on anyone in a similar situation. There is a God who gives hope, even to the hopeless! Rather, I share this so you can clearly see that living by this motto, will hardly deliver to you what was promised; instead, it will most certainly provide what you most dread.

One of the wisest kings to have walked the earth put it this way...

Dishonest money dwindles away, but whoever gathers money little by little makes it grow. (Proverbs 13:11)

Isn't that the truth?!

IN REALITY, WHAT IS THE RESULT OF LIVING BY THIS MOTTO?

I think it's pretty clear! By now you know as well as I do that the outcome of abiding by this motto is very different from what was originally intended. Members of traditional pyramid schemes go in expecting that in a short time they'll become filthy rich, but it only takes a bit of research to know that such members end up not only far from rich, but regretful of the time and resources wasted. It's nothing new. And, in fact, for those who do 'make it', you find that they've had to undergo all sorts of unwholesome practices—neglecting family, lying to others, exploiting friendships—in order to climb the ladder, often accompanied by a guilt that is not easily erased.

So, bringing it back to the streets, it's pretty clear what the result is. A criminal record is quite standard, especially if selling drugs has or would be your method of choice in order to get this money. And, sadly, as you most likely already know, this is the most accessible option on the streets.

But that's not all. Accompanying the criminal record is the *beef*[1] and constant paranoia—oh, you thought there wouldn't be any mental impact! As you start making some money, almost immediately you become aware that you can lose it just as fast. Remember that passage from Proverbs 13:11? You start to realise that, just like yourself, there are others who have bought into the same lie, and to them, you are an easy target, especially

---

1   Conflict that takes place on the streets between different and sometimes the same gang. *See Street Terms for more.*

if you're young and in the lower ranks of the streets pyramid.

The number of stories I've heard of young boys who have gone '*country*' (county lines) only to get robbed and end up in debt and hiding! This is how the paranoia sets in, not to forget the reality check that at any moment the police can be at your door. This is also when for some, the consumption and subsequent addiction to drugs among other substances starts to kick in.

But, unfortunately, that's not all! As is the case for many, they start to make some money—they buy the new trainers, secure the car (when of age), stash some savings, pose in pictures with bundles of cash—it's as if they've grasped success. But, sadly for them, this only furthers the delusion. Instead of recognising the folly of their ways, this 'taste' of money leaves them trapped—trapped within the pyramid, trapped on the streets. They move higher and higher through the ranks, only to be given a hefty, soul-wrenching jail sentence when caught (as I've sadly witnessed) or more brutally their life is taken.

It still hurts when I think of John who I've known for a long time. We used to play together when we were younger, and in our teens, I'd probably say I was deeper into the streets pyramid scheme than he was. While I was out of the country, he continued to 'progress'. He was making more money from the drugs and soon enough he was posting pictures in cars that I'd hardly even seen on the streets of London. Not only that, but John was also now rubbing shoulders with some of the older guys we looked up to. In fact, it was like they started looking up to him, even though he was much younger than they were. Some would say he was winning,

---

2   A location, usually outside the main city, where drug distribution takes place. *See Street Terms for more.*

but deep down it was clear he was trapped. And, indeed, it all came crashing down when it was sadly reported that he had been sentenced to over ten years in jail for trafficking illegal substances on a large scale. That's why I hate this myth!

> *How useless to spread a net where every bird can see it! These men lie in wait for their own blood; they ambush only themselves!* (Proverbs 1:17-18)

This is the reality of living by the motto: money over everything!

REALITY CHECK

Now do you see how the guys are selling you a dream? Can you see more clearly the trap that is right before you? Living by this motto will only bring loss—lost time, lost opportunities to invest elsewhere and, in some cases, loss of life. Your life is worth more.

But as with every myth, there is an opposing and clear truth. I came to understand it wasn't money over everything, but rather, Kingdom over everything. Let me share more with you in the next chapter.

MONEY OVER EVERYTHING VS. SEEK FIRST THE KINGDOM—PART 2

2

WHAT IS THE SOLUTION TO THIS MYTH, 'Money over everything'? Well, for one, it definitely doesn't mean that we should act like money or the things it can attain are irrelevant. We've all seen the struggle that a lack of finances can produce and also the benefits one can enjoy when it's abundant—so that's certainly not my argument. Rather, the solution to this myth is a replacement of your master!

A NEW MASTER—GOD OR MONEY?

'Master, you say? I'm my own boss, I serve no one!' If you were anything like me in my teens, that would be the comment running through my mind as I read this. But, yes, there was no typo—I say it again—a replacement of your master is the only solution! In the New Testament, God says the following:

> *Don't you know that when you offer yourselves to someone as obedient slaves, you are slaves of the one you obey ...* (Romans 6:16)

Very simply, your master is the one you obey. Or, to put it in other terms, show me the one thing you give yourself to the most, and I'll show you who your master is. For many on the streets, and most likely for you, money is the master. It was for me! It was the thing that directed my steps. Everything revolved around money.

What determines how successful you are? What gives you validation? What measures your worth? You already know the answer and, sadly, this is true on and off the streets. The truth is every time you repeat that myth, whether consciously or subconsciously, you give money (your master) more reign in your life. And, if you haven't heard it said before, I'll leave it here for your sake: 'Money is an excellent slave, but a terrible master.'

'Well, who do I replace my master with?' You ask. You need God, the Creator of the Universe, to be your new Master. Not only will He provide for your needs, but more than that, He will reveal His purposes for your life, the very reason why you were made. You see, up until this point, you might have thought that money was your greatest need—the streets and society have done well to make you believe that. But I want to let you know at this moment that your greatest need is actually God—knowing Him through Jesus and understanding why He made you.

> *When he had finished speaking, he said to Simon, "Put out into deep water, and let down the nets for a catch." Simon answered, "Master, we've worked hard all night and haven't caught anything. But because you say so, I will let down the nets." When they had done so, they caught such a large number of fish that their nets began to break. So they signalled their partners in the other boat to come and help them, and they came and filled both boats so*

> *full that they began to sink. When Simon Peter saw this, he fell at Jesus' knees and said, "Go away from me, Lord; I am a sinful man!" For he and all his companions were astonished at the catch of fish they had taken, and so were James and John, the sons of Zebedee, Simon's partners. Then Jesus said to Simon, "Don't be afraid; from now on you will fish for people."* (Luke 5:4-10)

Notice in the above passage from the Bible, Jesus meets Peter and his partners going about their daily work, trying to earn a living through fishing. Fishermen were your average Joe's in that day.

Now of all the humans that have walked the face of this earth, Jesus ranks first in terms of His expression of love; so it would be wise to watch and see how He treats others. If money were our greatest need, you would have thought that after Jesus helped them secure the greatest catch of their lives—that would have made them great profit—His job was done. But notice Jesus doesn't stop there, because life does not consist in the abundance of our possessions (hint: there is more to life than money!).

After miraculously providing for them, Jesus provides Peter with a new job, and a new mission, one that finds its meaning in His Kingdom[1]. With this miracle, it's as if Jesus was letting Peter know, 'Look, I can easily supply you with the things you need, but what's that worth if you don't know Me or the reason I made you?' Have you considered that before?

---

[1] The Kingdom of God is another term for God's order and reign. It's also a state of living in God's righteousness, peace and joy here on earth because you have accepted Jesus in your life. *See Bible Terms for more.*

LIFE IS MORE THAN MONEY

That is the real trade-off—chase money and guarantee yourself an unfulfilled life or let God be your Master and watch how He moulds you into the person He intended you to be. And why is that? Because you were not formed by God to trust in money, but to trust in Him! That's the crux of the matter, and these verses will bring some clarity to that.

> *No one can serve two masters. Either you will hate the one and love the other, or you will be devoted to the one and despise the other. You cannot serve both God and money. Therefore I tell you, do not worry about your life, what you will eat or drink; or about your body, what you will wear. Is not life more than food, and the body more than clothes?* (Matthew 6:24-25)

Here, Jesus makes it clear that the real reason 'money over everything' (why we serve money) speaks to us is because we're worried about our lives. As Jesus puts it, we're worried about what we're going to eat, drink and wear. At first, it doesn't come across like that when you hear the slogan used—sounds more like ambition or hunger. In fact, I never saw it this way until I became a follower of Jesus. But, dig a little deeper, and you'll find that at the root of those who parrot this myth is a whole heap of worry about the future: 'I don't want to be broke,' 'I'm going to be left behind,' 'I won't be loved or respected if I don't have money,' 'My life won't count for anything without money.' Whatever you name it, one thing is sure: worry and fear are at the root.

I remember coming back from Nigeria—after being shipped out—and noticing that the guys I used to chill with had surpassed me in terms of clothes, access to cars and other things. The thought lingered whether I could catch up with them if I went back to making money the way I used to on the streets; but these were all rooted in fear and insecurity. I know for some who return home from jail that this is a frequent reality. But I'm thankful I didn't go down that path and that my fear of feeling 'left behind' didn't drive me back to chasing money. By then I knew my life was worth much more.

In fact, as Jesus states, not only is our life worth more, but He says universally, that life itself is not made for us to be devoted to money or the things it can get us. It's like a person who goes to a party and all they are focused on is the cake—isn't the party more than the cake?! You get the point. So, if this was true for me, it's also true for you. But do you believe? Well, if you don't just yet, that's fine because there is more. Jesus gives us—for free—two examples from everyday life of how having God as your Master can save you from worry and slavery to money.

> *Look at the birds of the air; they do not sow or reap or store away in barns, and yet your heavenly Father feeds them. Are you not much more valuable than they? Can any one of you by worrying add a single hour to your life? And why do you worry about clothes? See how the flowers of the field grow. They do not labour or spin. Yet I tell you that not even Solomon in all his splendour was dressed like one of these. If that is how God clothes the grass of the field, which is here today and tomorrow is thrown into the fire, will he not much more clothe you—you of little faith?* (Matthew 6:26-30)

Are you catching this? Let's start with the birds! I don't know if you've ever stopped to observe birds. Living in the city we don't tend to. But in this passage, Jesus wants us to learn something about God and our value to Him by considering the nature of a bird. While birds go from place to place to source food to eat, they have neither the ability nor capacity to plant a field full of seeds, wait for the crops to harvest and then gather them, eat some and store a portion away for a later date. It's too complex!

That's the equivalent of someone today utilising their building skills over thirty days to refurbish a bathroom (sowing), receiving payment upon completion and then enjoying the rewards (reaping), and saving anything left over for the months ahead (investing). Birds just can't do that. And yet, knowing this, let me ask you, do you find dead pigeons lying all around England? No; why? Because, as Jesus lets us know, our Heavenly Father feeds them. He goes out of His way to provide for them.

How about flowers? You may not say this out loud, but you and I know they are beautiful. It's why someone can be in a terrible state and you bring in a vase full of colourful flowers, almost immediately, they brighten up. Beauty does that! Yet I don't know about you, but I've never come across flowers that make clothes for themselves or work in order to afford the type of 'clothing' they possess. Again, it's not possible. Why? Because, as Jesus tells us, our Heavenly Father is the One who goes out of His way to clothe them like that.

YOU'RE MORE VALUABLE THAN YOU REALISE

Are you now getting the point? God, our Heavenly Father, feeds, clothes, and takes care of things that are worth much less than you and me. If He does this for common birds and flowers, will He not do this for those whom He created to reflect Him?

Will He not do it for you, if only you trusted Him and gave over your fears?

Have you ever seen parents who go out of their way to help the homeless, while their very own children are also homeless and hungry? Not at all. And this is what Jesus is letting us know. Our Heavenly Father not only values us but desires to take care of us. Therefore, you don't need to serve money or live your life constantly trying to chase it, only to find out in the end that not only did you waste your life, but you rejected the God who sought to free you from this slavery.

> So do not worry, saying, "What shall we eat?" or "What shall we drink?" or "What shall we wear?" For the pagans run after all these things, and your heavenly Father knows that you need them. But seek first his kingdom and his righteousness[2], and all these things will be given to you as well. (Matthew 6:31-33)

So, instead of trying to align your life with this myth from the streets, listen to the truth from God. He's inviting you to trust Him and hand over every fear, worry and insecurity you possess, especially when it comes to money. The passage asks this question, 'What will I eat, drink or wear?' But equally it could be, 'What will I do without money from drugs?' or 'What will people say if I wore the same trainers for a year?'

Whatever the worry, I can assure you that there is a God who sees and knows and, most importantly, is longing to help. Jesus' encouragement to you is this: don't be an unbeliever, who spends their life trying to answer these endless questions

---

2   Living in right relationship with God. This means we live justly, honestly, and faithfully according to God's instruction. *See Bible Terms for more.*

of worry. Instead trust (believe) in our God and Father who lacks nothing, knows exactly what you need and promises to supply just that!

FOCUS ON GOD'S KINGDOM

You might now be asking yourself, 'Alright, cool. If God will provide for me, then what am I to do with my time and energy?' It's a great question, because once you mentally stop chasing money, you find that there's a freedom to focus on other things. And Jesus answers this question clearly towards the end of the previous passage: *Seek first His [God's] kingdom and his righteousness, and all these things will be given to you as well.*

Though the title of this chapter is 'Seek First the Kingdom'—the truth that opposes the streets lie—I had to spend time emphasising the need for you to replace your Master. You see, you can only start seeking God's Kingdom once you learn how to acknowledge Him as Master, and trust Him for everything! It's like skydiving. Divers will only commit to jumping out of a plane once they trust that the parachute will bring them down safely (that not happening being their greatest fear).

If you can trust God with taking care of your needs financially, then you can trust Him with everything else. As we've just seen, money is the choice of worship for many—including those on the streets—because they're worried about their lives and make money their saviour. But, once God becomes your Master and the answer for your life, then you live your life to represent Him. Think representing the *ends*[3], but on a greater

---

3   The area one is from, which is usually deprived. *See Street Terms for more.*

scale, representing the eternal Kingdom of God, pushing forward, and advancing His cause right where you live.

Rather than asking 'What will I wear?' you now ask, 'What did God create me for?' because you know that the previous question is already covered. These passages from God's Word shed some light on this:

> *For we are God's handiwork, created in Christ Jesus to do good works, which God prepared in advance for us to do.* (Ephesians 2:10)

> *And whatever you do, whether in word or deed, do it all in the name of the Lord Jesus, giving thanks to God the Father through him.* (Colossians 3:17)

> *Whatever you do, work at it with all your heart, as working for the Lord, not for human masters, since you know that you will receive an inheritance from the Lord as a reward. It is the Lord Christ you are serving.* (Colossians 3:23-24)

> *Therefore, my dear brothers and sisters, stand firm. Let nothing move you. Always give yourselves fully to the work of the Lord, because you know that your labour in the Lord is not in vain.* (1 Corinthians 15:58)

Take these words in! Seeking God's Kingdom, as you can see in these passages, involves representing Jesus in all you do. You can be a student, electrician, plumber, business owner, musician, personal trainer, banker—you name it! But no longer do you live to glorify or 'big up' yourself. Rather, you do everything to big up your Saviour and Master. The streets become a thing of the past because you're now part of a larger entity—God's Kingdom. You start to recognise that God had a plan and purpose for your life. Nothing is by coincidence, and He intends to refine and utilise your skills, gifts and person to bring praise to Jesus.

No longer do you chase money and worry whether your endeavours are going to amount to anything. Instead, you have confidence in all that you do for Jesus, because no matter what anyone says or how insignificant you feel you are, everything done for God's Kingdom will last forever.

Why? Because of all that you see in God's world today, only that which is done for His Kingdom will stand the test of time. God invites you to this life. Remember, He says that, if you accept it, all those needs that you previously worried about will be supplied to you as well. What a God we serve!

I HAVE SEEN HIM DO IT

I'm going to close this chapter out with a personal story which highlights the above. By this time, I had been off the streets for quite a while and, in fact, I was working within banking. I was married and recently had a child, and so this job that God gave me and in which I represented Him, was a great support for my family. However, through my relationship with Jesus, I started to sense that as part of God's plan for my life at that moment, He wanted me to leave banking in order to give myself to sharing His message—the Gospel—in a different capacity.

At first, as you can imagine, I was shaken to my bones. I wondered how I would take care of my family and pay my mortgage. But, after about a year of speaking with God in prayer, handing over fears to Him, and reflecting on passages like the ones shared in this chapter, my wife and I decided that we must take this step.

Why? Because we recognised that our lives were made for more—God's eternal Kingdom—and that Jesus could be trusted. It wasn't easy, but I can tell you that we never begged for food. He took care of us—we could still pay our mortgage! But more than that, He used us to bless others and advance His Kingdom right where we lived.

So, my encouragement to you is not to worry about the decision you may need to make if you're going to leave this myth behind. As we've covered in this chapter, remember 'money over everything' is the streets counterfeit for true purpose. Only in God's Kingdom will you find true fulfilment!

SCAN TO WATCH THE END OF CHAPTERS 1-2 VIDEO

Alternatively, search www.safehavenprints.com/tsvtk12

VIOLENCE IS THE WAY VS. SEEK PEACE

3

I'M GOING TO BEGIN BY ASKING YOU A QUESTION: Do you listen to street rap? I certainly did while I was on the streets, and though times and artists have changed to some degree, the content of the music is very much the same. It is the same stuff but just a different era! You might be wondering why I am asking such a question, so let me break it down.

CHECK THE LYRICS

I was not simply asking whether you've heard the beat of these songs, but whether you listen to and process what is being said on the beat. There is a big difference because, while many—even those who are not on the streets—can vibe to these rhythms, few actually take time to consider what is being said and why.

I remember reading out the lyrics of a popular song by a UK female drill artist at a gathering of young people at my church. Let us just say there were many stunned and embarrassed faces as I broke down the meaning of some of the lines. Maybe they were only realising them for the first time, maybe not; but it was an eye opener for most.

Now I know that the subject of whether street rap/drill music drives violence and beef on the streets is a touchy one. You may have an opinion. I know I sure do. But in asking this initial question, the hope is that my answer will shed light on this subject and, more importantly, expose the myth I will be focusing on in this chapter: Violence is the Way.

What benefit did you reap at that time from the things you are now ashamed of? Those things result in death! (Romans 6:21)

You see, the rap artist is usually portrayed as a storyteller who is artistically reporting on what is happening in the area. A neutral storyteller, I should add. That emphasis is very important.

But let's explore this reasoning just a little. Imagine if some police officers aggressively stopped and searched one of your friends, and in the process, one officer hit your friend's head on the wall resulting in a concussion. That would be a terrible situation. But do you know what would be even more disgusting? The officer reporting the incident and, instead of showing remorse, saying to his colleagues, 'I showed that young man who's boss when I bashed his head on the wall.' Can you see my point?

On the one hand the police officer is clearly reporting what happened. But, on the other, his retelling of it glorifies the brutal actions that led to your friend's injury. It shows that there is generally no neutral ground when recounting events. In other words, the storyteller is either going to glorify and justify those things they report on or disapprove of and denounce them.

Now I'm sure you can guess which side the majority of street rap sits on? That's why the above passage is fitting because, rather than expressing shame and regret for the violence rampant on the streets, the lyrics take pride in the acts performed. This is the way artists have intentionally chosen to recount these events. The very things that result in death on the streets are paraded by such artists as badges of honour—a feeling completely at odds with the scripture verse above. Why is that? Put simply, the myth on the streets is that value and reputation is earned and maintained by being violent: violence is the way. And, sadly, many believe it—I once did!

THE VICIOUS CYCLE OF EARNING STRIPES

Earning your stripes is what we were made to believe growing up. In practice, this meant responding with violence towards anyone who disrespected you or the area. I'm sure the streets have also sold you this myth as well. This is why street rap is the way it is, a musical expression of the myths from the streets. Some artists have already lived out this myth and so to show their 'authenticity', they will ensure their lyrics are spiked with the violence they themselves perpetrated.

Other artists, knowing full well they have not lived that life, adopt similar themed lyrics as a way of building reputation and gaining acceptance from those who subscribe to the myth. And street rap thrives because many have already been convinced that violence is the way to 'success'. So, of course, street rap can and does trigger violence in our society; but street rap is what it is because the gang member has believed in a lie! But enough about the music for now.

> *Although they know God's righteous decree that those who do such things deserve death, they not only continue to do these very things but also approve of those who practise them.* (Romans 1:32)

Back to earning stripes, this is what we were taught, which is also described as 'putting in work'. But do you know what it does to you if you become hoodwinked by this myth? It puts you on a path of violence that deep down you already know is wrong. But, strangely, like the prior passage states, not only do you continue down that path but gradually you begin to approve of and respect others who live exactly the same way.

A dangerous cycle, indeed. How? Because, whether you realise it or not, you are actually on a path to destruction. This is because your violence is only as 'good' as your last episode. Am I lying? The streets may have praised you yesterday because you pushed over a boy who was from a rival area, but you know as well as I do that tomorrow that praise will be gone. The streets will require you to go further down the path to receive their praise again. You need to work to get promoted! No wonder nowadays you can find olders in the area recounting with a sigh that in their day people just used fists; now the young ones are running around with knives and guns. What they fail to see, however, is that the young ones are in the same destructive cycle as they were—trying to earn their stripes!

If you don't put in the work, you'll be considered sub-par, and no one likes to feel sub-par, inferior and cast aside. I'm sure you don't. That's why for some the streets become almost some type of safe place. Whereas in school, at home or in wider society you may feel neglected and inferior, the streets—in a deceptive sort of way—tell you you're valued and superior. However, this is not because they recognise you were made by a God who formed you with worth and meaning, rather it's because your violence and "work" is earning a great reputation for both you and your area.

Maybe this resonates with you. It sure did for me because

I was drawn in by this. I wanted to feel valued, and the streets tricked me into thinking this was the sure way. That pride and fake worth is intoxicating, I know. It's why you end up saying to yourself subconsciously, 'I must never be violated. But if I am, I will surely do even more harm to whoever tries to disrespect me or the gang.' Because, if you don't, or if you ever found it in yourself to forgive and not pay back whoever wronged you, you would be demoted, kicked out and sent back down that imaginary ladder. No one wants that, so you are almost certainly sucked into a life of violence and more violence. This is the definition of bondage!

Do not envy the violent or choose any of their ways. (Proverbs 3:31)

The violence of the wicked will destroy them, because they refuse to do justice. (Proverbs 21:7 NKJV)

Knowing all this then, why do you still go down this path? Why is the news still sadly filled with scenes of young lives perishing? Well, as we noted in the Introduction, our hearts are sincerely diseased. Without help from God, they side with those things that lead to death, over and above the things that bring true life. And nothing is clearer than with this myth: violence is the way. Let me show you how with this quick thought experiment.

According to this myth, who is at the top of the ladder? Isn't it the person the streets would consider to be a legend? If so, picture that person who holds that title from your area for a moment. Do you remember the reputation they possessed? Now ask yourself, where are they? Sadly, in my area that person is no longer alive; he didn't even live to see thirty. What is worse is that this answer, for the most part, would be similar all across the UK if this thought experiment was repeated. This is why God warns us in the scripture before not to envy the violent, for this myth only leads one way!

SEEKING PEACE IS THE ANTIDOTE

So, which way should I go, you ask? By this point in the book you may already know the answer, but in case you do not, it is God's way. His ways are always the best. God's way involves seeking peace with our enemies, which is very different from what you and I were taught on the streets. Seeking peace was and still is looked at as a sign of weakness. But what we fail to see is that seeking peace is the only way to counter this myth that has greatly destroyed countless lives on the streets. And I am glad to write that, in some part, I have actually been able to see this myth destroyed.

I grew up in Lewisham Borough in South East London, and coming up everyone knew that we had a dislike of those from Southwark Borough, particularly Peckham. The beef and the accompanying violence between both areas started long before I was even a teen in the mid 2000s. By then, numerous people had been stabbed, some had been shot at, others died, while most were on edge—because the guiding principle between both sides was violence all the way.

Now I am sure there was a valid reason—some type of offence—for why this conflict started, though it does not mean that one should condone what followed. Conflict does not always have to lead to violence. Evil is always disproportionate, and the streets are no different. But the sad thing is that growing up none of my peers could articulate exactly why we did not like each other. We just took it for granted, much like we treat the oxygen God continually supplies.

Despite this awful background though, I was amazed to see through social media in the late 2000s—I was not in the UK at this time—pictures of members from both sides posing together. It was a complete shock for me, because only a few years before, the very same people would have been plotting and scheming how to do damage to one another, as was expected. Add to that the obvious fact that these men, who had come together, would have been well aware that people they cared about had been hurt or even murdered by associates of those they were now making peace with. So, you can imagine why I was shocked.

Seeking peace is not encouraged on the streets. It's not easy or natural for us, especially when the offence runs deep. But it is possible, as you can see, and I am thankful that it could happen in my area. Many lives have been spared through this truce, and long may it continue!

PEACE DOESN'T MAKE YOU WEAK

But you may say these guys who were involved in this truce were soft. How could they make peace with people who had wronged them? I wish they could answer for themselves in this book. Without that though, and with no knowledge of their heartfelt motives, I'd ask you this question: according to who are they soft? The myth of the streets? The same myth that destroys your boys—who you care about—with no end in sight? This is why the streets need God's way, and according to Him seeking peace is not soft or weak. Rather, it is a reflection of His mercy, love and forgiving character. These are the very things we are all called to mirror, as those made in His likeness.

> *But I tell you, love your enemies and pray for those who persecute you, that you may be children of your Father in heaven. He causes his sun to rise on the evil and the good, and sends rain on the righteous and the unrighteous.* (Matthew 5:44-45)

You see, what you have to understand is that God gets your frustration. What do I mean by that? I mean that God knows what it is like to be offended, to be wronged. Isn't this one of the key reasons for the violence on the streets—retaliating over an offence? God gets it, for He is wronged daily! The difference between the streets and our Creator, however, is that He does not live by this myth, but instead walks in the truth. He is the Truth!

In the Bible passage just quoted, Jesus breaks this down for us, pointing to the weather to understand God's character. Jesus tells those who choose to follow Him to love their enemies and pray for those who persecute them. Outrageous, shocking, I know! But why? How can they do this? Because daily, Jesus Christ our Mediator in Heaven does the very same thing for countless people who have wronged him (see Hebrews 9:15, Hebrews 7:25).

Tell me, would you expect someone you violated on the streets yesterday to help you out tomorrow? We do not even need to answer that question, because our natural bent for revenge makes this a rhetorical one. And yet, the God who created you, who you have wronged through living by the myths of the streets and breaking His good and perfect law through sin, does not withhold His summer sun from shining on you or stop the rain from falling on the soil that produces the food you eat.

In other words, though you deserve God's retaliation for all your wrongdoing right this moment, He instead chooses daily to show you His kindness. In fact, it says elsewhere in the Scriptures, that His rich kindness is intended to lead you to repentance and peace with Him (Romans 2:4). I wonder whether you have ever realised this before. I once hadn't.

Now you have got to help me answer this question. Is God weak? Is God soft? Is He weak or soft for loving you, His enemy (note: an enemy is one who actively opposes someone)? Far from it! God is strong, mighty, powerful. One of the main ways He demonstrates this is through His ability to simultaneously endure patiently with His enemies and work to make them friends.

GOD MADE PEACE WITH US

You may say, 'Well, shouldn't it be easy for God to love and forgive those who have wronged Him?' Yes, you're right, because He is more loving than you and I. But what you fail to see is that because He is more loving—in fact, He is Love—it means He also hates evil much more than we do. In other words, wronging God is the greatest offence any human could commit. It means that God seeking peace with His enemies—you and I—is a much greater act than gangs from Lewisham making peace with those from Southwark, or even the Crips making peace with the Bloods!

> *You see, at just the right time, when we were still powerless, Christ died for the ungodly. Very rarely will anyone die for a righteous person, though for a good person someone might possibly dare to die. But God demonstrates his own love for us in this: While we were still sinners, Christ died for us.* (Romans 5:6-8)

This is what the Cross is all about—the pictures, the chains, the structures outside church buildings. The Cross is God's way of making peace with His enemies, you and me, through His Son, Jesus Christ, suffering and dying on it for our sakes. Now I am sure you might be asking, why and how did this bring about peace? It's a good question, and it will be addressed fully in the last chapter.

Put simply for now, in just the same way that an unpaid debt creates a divide between the borrower and the lender, my sin and your sin is the unpaid debt that created a divide between God and us. As you can imagine, peace can only happen once that debt is paid back or cancelled. Now on the Cross—as planned before all time—Jesus made peace by cancelling and paying off our sin-debt in full, by His death. The only currency that could satisfy such a debt owed to God was a life unstained and untouched by sin. And guess what? Of all humanity, only Jesus, the Son of God, was able to provide that. He did so willingly for you and me, in spite of our blatant rebellion. The passage says *'While we were sinners …'* He made peace through His blood on the Cross.

Can you see what God did? Look at the strength and love of Jesus—to suffer in the place of His enemies in order that they may have peace with God. He died so that you may live! Now can you see why 'Violence Is the Way' is a complete falsehood? While the streets train you into believing that violence and more of it will grant you power, notoriety and one over your enemies, the God of all power, fame and glory for all eternity, laid down His life to seek peace with His enemies. I remember when this hit me, it changed everything in my world, in particular, the way I viewed those who had done me wrong.

PRACTICE WHAT YOU PREACH

I am going to end this chapter with a personal story because I can assure you that I don't write without personal context, especially this chapter. When I became a Christian, I left the streets behind me—well, I thought I did. It wasn't until I was at this event at my church, where all those in attendance were asked whether they harboured unforgiveness towards anyone. This is because Jesus teaches His followers to forgive and release, given He has forgiven us of much more. He says it's like failing to let someone off a £50 debt, when you've just been let off a £500,000 one.

Jesus tells the story of a servant whose master forgave a huge debt and then caught him threatening someone who owed him peanuts.

> *Then the master called the servant in. "You wicked servant," he said, "I cancelled all that debt of yours because you begged me to. Shouldn't you have had mercy on your fellow servant just as I had on you?"* (Matthew 18:32-33)

But in the room at this church event, you could hear some people crying, and I just thought, 'Damn, people must hold some deep grudges inside.' I remember sitting there and thinking, 'No not me, I've made peace with everyone,' until an older lady approached me and asked whether I had anyone I needed to forgive. I said, no, but for some reason she wasn't letting up and so she said, 'Why don't you ask God, and He may bring something to remembrance?' So I thought, 'Why not?'

Believe me, when I did this, I was immediately reminded of the night I was bottled after a party as a teenager. I had flashbacks of the situation. How I felt, who I was with and ultimately who did it. I was filled with a mixture of emotions—anger, fear and sadness. In that moment, all I could think about was the anger I had towards this guy Martin who did it. I thought I had dealt with it. I thought I had forgiven him. But I hadn't! I had to ponder whether if, given the chance, would I do to him what he had done to me? I thank God for Jesus because in those moments of praying, I was reminded of how He had forgiven me of so much more. So how could I harbour revenge against Martin despite what he did!? In the end, I left that event lighter and, funnily enough, even wishing I could see him so I could let him know I had forgiven him.

Well, God has a way of answering prayers. Around five years later I was visiting one of my old friends who happened to be in jail. On the visit, guess who I saw also visiting? No, not the Martin who bottled me. But Timmy who told Martin to bottle me because it was my friends and his who had initially started this conflict in the first place.

When I first spotted Timmy and his associates, I remember thinking, 'Oh, oh, what's going to happen? God what are You doing?' For some reason, I knew that God was in this and also with me, and that I was not heading for a beat down. Towards the end of the visit, when all visitors had to vacate, Timmy and I locked eyes and we started talking. I told him that I had forgiven him for what he did all those years ago—I still have the scar to show for it. I even told him about the experience I had at that church event, where God brought to remembrance everything that happened. He also apologised and shared the usual stance—after growing up—that we were all just silly back in the day. Isn't that the truth! If only the young ones could catch this right now!

But as I drove home that day, I just had to ponder and ask what all this was about. From that event years after becoming a Christian to that meeting at the prison. And it became very clear to me that God was showing—up, close and personal through my life experiences—how invested He is in seeking peace. He is a God of reconciliation, a God who seeks peace and desires that ungodly divisions are healed and overcome, rather than perpetuated by this evil myth. He wanted to heal me; that I understood. But what I didn't expect was that He would orchestrate an encounter just so I could make peace with those I once considered enemies. This is what Jesus does—makes peace—and it is exactly what He wants to do on these streets. Life instead of death; peace instead of violence!

SCAN TO WATCH THE END OF CHAPTER 3 VIDEO

Alternatively, search www.safehavenprints.com/tsvtk3

NO SNITCHING VS. EXPOSE THE WORKS OF DARKNESS

4

THIS CHAPTER IS A WEIGHTY ONE and we are going straight into it. Although all the other myths may have contributed in some way to who you've become, the concept of 'no snitching' is one of the major beliefs and reasons why violence and death on our streets persist. Do you think I'm exaggerating? Why don't you read this quote from one of the wisest men who has ever lived and I'm sure you'll probably want to reconsider your opinion.

> *When the sentence for a crime is not quickly carried out, people's hearts are filled with schemes to do wrong.* (Ecclesiastes 8:11)

Isn't that the truth? No snitching comes in as the myth of all myths that the streets indoctrinate every wannabe gang member with. In other words, not informing others, particularly the authorities, of evil acts witnessed. You know this is true, isn't it? I learnt how to say 'no comment' to the police long before I learnt how to get into university and, ironically, long before I had even been arrested for a crime. Imagine that!

In fact, I'm sure you know quite well that even the non-participant who happens to be from the area also abides by this code. And in my experience, even certain ex-gang members, who would publicly say they are not associated with any gang, find it hard to shrug off this myth in their own lives. Out of all the other beliefs on the streets, no snitching is clearly the one that has the strongest hold over most participants, even when they are no longer active.

Why is that? Here's my take.

NO SNITCHING IS ROOTED IN FEAR

It's due to fear and pride. These are the twin reasons why this stronghold of no snitching still survives. It was the same in my generation and it will be the same in the years to come, unless you allow God's truth to set you free.

> *Fear of man will prove to be a snare, but whoever trusts in the Lord is kept safe.* (Proverbs 29:25)

So, let's start with fear. I never wanted to be called a snitch during my time on the streets. You could call me anything else, but don't call me a snitch! Why? Well, pride is part of it, which I will touch on after, but the fear of what others would do or say if I was known to be a snitch tormented me. Let's be honest; it's not an easy life for someone who is known to be a snitch. And you know, that it has not changed over the years. Darkness never wants to be exposed to the light!

Such a person would be the brunt of constant jokes and cussing, even from those who did not have a reputation on par with them before snitching. Most of their friendships would be disbanded, as those around would no longer trust them with their dirty deeds. And it's not unlikely for the ones who they once considered 'brothers' to turn on them and be the first to assault them violently just to prove a point. How do I know this? Because it's the mindset I once had—the 'right' one if you are trying to live according to the myths of the streets. And last, but certainly not the least, some have even lost their lives for the act of snitching.

So, trust me when I say I understand why you would not be comfortable going against the pack. The fear of retaliation and all that comes with it is a heavy price to pay. But, equally so, is the weight of witnessing the great injustices that take place on the streets. (We will touch on this point a bit later.) Nevertheless, the sentence of death—physical and social (friendships)—is a powerful force wielded on the streets to allow all sorts of evil to prosper, while keeping shut the mouths of those who know deep down in their souls that it is not right. You'd be surprised, but this slavery to the fear of death did not start on the streets, nor is it only gang members that are bound by it. As the passage below shows, this tactic of enslaving people through their fear of death has been in play for a while and it is only God who can set us free from it.

> *Since the children have flesh and blood, he [Jesus] too shared in their humanity so that by his death he might break the power of him who holds the power of death—that is, the devil—and free those who all their lives were held in slavery by their fear of death.* (Hebrews 2:14-15, emphasis added)

IT IS ALSO ROOTED IN PRIDE

But you may say, 'It's not because of fear of what the guys will do to me that I subscribe to no snitching. Rather I'm not a snitch because I'm not built that way.' As if not being a snitch comes with a medal that will grant you and your descendants honour in the years to come! But let's be honest, this is exactly what the streets teach us: somehow not snitching will enhance our reputation and add some sort of credibility to it. This is a lie though; in fact, it's pride. This is the second reason this myth finds fertile ground on the streets and in your heart.

Pride goes before destruction, a haughty spirit before a fall.
(Proverbs 16:18)

Imagine a business you have recently setup. Its value rises or falls depending on the expectations of future profits. Expect strong profits and the business' value goes up; expect the opposite and its value goes down. You get the gist. Well, no snitching and pride as it relates to the streets works in the very same way.

Instead of a business however, it's your own personal value—as judged by the streets—that's at stake. And instead of the amount of profit determining your value, it's your ability to keep your mouth closed—no snitching—that ensures you're viewed highly in the eyes of others. You snitch, your value falls; you don't, and it goes all the way up. Am I lying? And then we have pride urging you to do whatever it takes to maintain your worth. Who doesn't want to be seen in that light? But what's the cost of striving for value in this way? Years, and sometimes, decades languishing in jail, for a crime you did not commit (though you know who did). A family mourning a close relative while the true killer goes free. Last but not least, precious time away from your own family just so that your street credibility remains intact.

Though just an analogy, isn't this the reality of this myth? That is why the passage quoted above is so key, because, wherever pride is involved, destruction is not far behind. And what I have spelled out in the example above is not too far from the reality that some, on the streets, are currently living through. They sit in jail knowing full well that everything around them is crumbling; yet despite this, they are kept afloat by the false assurance of 'Well, my guys still love me.'

Pride prevented them from snitching and in return they have reaped destruction all around. The worst thing though is that, while the streets may applaud you right now, it's the very same people you're trying to impress who will turn around and disown you as their lives go on. In other words, trying to uphold your value through not snitching is a fruitless task, because either way everything heads south when you live by the myths of the streets.

THERE'S NO FRUIT

So, what are you to do? Because, though there is hope in Jesus, even for the one who is reading this in jail right now, I do not want this story to become your very own. What are you to do then? Look to God's word! What does He say? In this verse, He crushes this myth by saying:

> Have nothing to do with the fruitless deeds of darkness, but rather expose them (Ephesians 5:11, emphasis added).

Back to the business and investing analogy we mentioned just now. Would you accept a recommendation to invest in a start-up company that received a license to produce Blackberry phones? I certainly hope not. Blackberry themselves in 2022 stopped manufacturing their once famous device as they lost customers to the iPhone and other competitors. In essence, it became pointless to produce these phones as the end customer did not want them. I guess you don't have a Blackberry, do you!?

But why do I mention this—because it's very clear that investing in such a company is a fruitless pursuit, as it ultimately amounts to nothing but losses. And in the exact same way, God's truth describes the very things you seek to 'protect' by not snitching as fruitless! What could they be? How about the unsolved stabbing of a young man who was mistaken for an opponent from another area? What about the young girl and boy who are reported missing, though it's well known that they're in country operating the drug line? And how about the botched robbery that resulted in someone being shot?

These things and more, God says, have nothing to do with because they are futile and rooted in great darkness. I needed to hear this when I was younger. I knew many 'hood stories' of people who had used a gun and got away with it, used fake notes to purchase numerous items or swarmed a council estate with weapons and beat anyone they sighted. But what did it produce in me? Let's go back to Ecclesiastes 8:11: *When the sentence for a crime is not quickly carried out, people's hearts are filled with schemes to do wrong.* This was true in my life, because it only produced a heart filled with schemes to do wrong, and to perform more fruitless deeds of darkness.

I deceptively thought I could do whatever I wanted because no one was going to tell on me. There would be no justice. I told myself I could wreak havoc without any real consequence. As I said before, this is one of the key reasons why evil and crime persist in our communities. Those who should be off the streets are not, because those who are on the streets won't say anything. You may think you are being loyal, but all you are doing is bringing further damage to the community—making evil look good and good look evil, while the cycle of crime on the streets only continues.

EXPOSE THE DARKNESS

So again, what is to be done? Rather than not snitch, these deeds of darkness on the streets need to be exposed! They need to come into the light because, whenever darkness enters the light, it flees. But going back to what I mentioned earlier, fear is one of the major reasons why the latter never happens. That's why exposing these deeds of darkness starts by fearing God and not man! The streets, and a much greater enemy behind acts of evil, want to keep you muzzled out of your fear of death.

> *I tell you, my friends, do not be afraid of those who kill the body and after that can do no more. But I will show you whom you should fear: Fear him who, after your body has been killed, has authority to throw you into hell. Yes, I tell you, fear him.* (Luke 12:4-5)

Just as we need a new Master to be freed from the 'money over everything' myth, so too is a greater fear needed if you are going to be freed from 'no snitching'. In the passage above, Jesus makes very clear how this works. In essence, He tells us that we should fear the One who can do the most damage to us. That makes sense, right? But what He reveals is that, while you may think it's your boys or that no-nonsense older that deserves that fear and reverence, it is God our Creator, who alone should have that spot.

You see—though it's not a trivial matter—if you expose darkness, the absolute most that those from the area can do is kill you. And, as we've seen, the streets use death as a tool to enslave and silence you. But after that they can do nothing else. They have no power beyond the grave. With God, however, not only is life and death in His hands, but He alone has the authority to determine what happens to your soul after death. And trust me when I say, living by the myths of the streets will definitely not lead to a good place in this life or beyond.

THE GREATER FEAR

Let me give you an analogy to drive this home further. My wife and I manage a property and every so often tenants move out and we need to find new ones to rent the room. Now at times, the thought of not finding a tenant haunts me, in addition to the loss of income if the rent is not covered to pay for basic bills. That's fear!

Now I could choose to be afraid that the room will be empty, and so just let anyone move in for fear that we won't receive any rent for the coming month. Alternatively, I could be even more fearful that, by letting anyone in, I could receive a bad tenant who trashes the property and empties our pockets for months to come! As you can imagine, the latter fear quenches the first, and my perspective and therefore my actions shift to looking for a good tenant—despite the time taken—rather than just filling it with anyone.

It's the exact same when it comes to exposing the deeds of darkness. Though you are aware of what the guys can do, the above passage makes it crystal clear what God can do. The knowledge and acceptance of this truth can shift your perspective and give you confidence to side with God. So, you rise above your fear and expose the darkness of the streets, despite how you may be perceived by your boys. The fear of God certainly did that for me. That is exactly why I am writing this book—to expose the myths I was once sold. But it is worth noting that, while you should fear God because of the authority He holds over your life, when you come to know Him, you will find that your actions will be motivated by His great love for you as well as your fear (great respect) of Him. We will touch on this more in the last chapter of this book, so hold on!

But going back to where we were, do not forget this important point: God takes care of those who trust in Him. The second passage quoted in this chapter, Proverbs 29:25, speaks to the fact that fearing the guys from the area is a snare, a trap of sorts; but, when you trust in God, you are kept safe. Those who choose to walk with God are never alone, especially when exposing the darkness on the streets.

But what does it look like in practical terms to expose the darkness, and what will it produce? You may be thinking like those lines from the famous song 'Changes', 'Some things will never change, that's just the way it is.' So, let's start with the practical steps that can be taken.

TRANSATLANTIC SLAVERY WAS EXPOSED

I want to draw on past examples where God has exposed darkness in society because, though we live in a new era, some of the same principles apply. I'm sure you had to learn about the transatlantic slave trade when you were in school, possibly in history class. I sure did, though I never took it seriously.

But in my later years I took to reading about it. I became captivated by how a nation like the U.K that benefitted so greatly from this evil, produced home-grown opponents who managed to convince the nation to outlaw slavery. I'm not going to do an in-depth study here as there are other books and videos for that, but I want to highlight some of the practical steps that were taken, and show you how they can be transferred to exposing the streets.

First things first. Leading abolitionists like Thomas Clarkson, Granville Sharp and William Wilberforce exposed slavery by bringing it into God's light. It's one thing to make use of a flickering flashlight to light a room and it's completely another for the sun to light it up. God's law is like the sun, and these particular opponents to slavery made it very clear that enslaving other humans because of their ethnicity wasn't just an offence against humanity, but an offence against the God who made all people in His image with dignity and value. The streets need to know that its activity isn't just affecting the community, but that it's an offence against God Himself. He looks with displeasure at what the guys are doing and He is willing to act. Will you share the light of God with them?

Secondly, these men shared personal stories of the terrors of slavery—the beatings, how people were captured, families that were torn apart and other brutal things that I cannot mention here. These stories came from both those who were enslaved as well as ex-slave owners. The last part is crucial because the ex-slave masters were in essence 'self-snitching', that is, confessing and exposing their own contribution to the evil that had developed. We may know the song 'Amazing Grace', but what many of us do not know is that the composer John Newton was once a captain of a slave trading vessel, who saw the light of God's word, repented and then campaigned against this evil practice.

And notice they were now calling it evil, not good! Though other slave masters couldn't have cared less, some would have felt shame and regret because what was now being described as vile and corrupt was exactly what they were doing for a living. Imagine one of the olders you respected in the area coming to your school and confessing that he was in fact a *wasteman*[1] because of the very same things that earned him respect in the first place. What would that do for the next generation? Maybe that older is you?

Also linked to the last point, is the use of social media. In those days, they didn't have Instagram, TikTok or X as you can imagine. But it was the print media that was widely used to expose the evils of slavery and change the minds of the masses right here in this very country. One book that did just that was by an ex-slave, Olaudah Equiano. He wrote of his experiences of being captured in West Africa and all he endured—let's just say it went viral in his time, and many hearts were challenged and changed as a result.

The same can be done in exposing the streets. You can utilise YouTube and make videos revealing the realities of being active—the sleepless nights, the PTSD, the betrayal by your very own. And, if you are artistic, how about releasing music that doesn't sugar coat the street lifestyle but instead teaches the audience, particularly the youth, that this is not the life they want to have, despite all the glorifying of it by former members in order to rake in money from sales? I know quite a few people who already use music to expose the darkness of the streets in just this way—and it's bearing fruit!

But lastly, and definitely not everything, was the role of the police at sea. As you can imagine, to stop a slave ship from taking enslaved people from West Africa to other parts of the world, you needed a strong presence at sea to combat these traders. And that is exactly what the U.K did with the West African Squadron, who were part of the Royal Navy stationed around the coast of West Africa.

---

[1] Someone those on the streets look down on because they don't live up to their standards for one reason or another. See *Street Terms for more.*

THE STREETS vs THE KINGDOM

THIS IS HOW IT RELATES

But where's the application to the streets? Well, this Squadron, while skilled in their own right, certainly could not tackle this evil alone. No, they probably also received help from locals and maybe even from ex-traders/slavers who had witnessed firsthand the horrors of slavery and were sickened by the destruction to human life. Similar to what happens on the streets, they cooperated with the police in order to catch the perpetrators.

Now you may ask, though I hope not, why did the people associated with the trade snitch? I would respond by asking, would you still want the transatlantic slave trade to be a present reality? Neither did they! So why not cooperate with the police—provided you were actually a witness to a crime—so that the streets and its destruction to human life in its current form can be dismantled? This is a space where organisations that serve as middlemen between the police and ex-gang members can play a role, in spite of the lack of trust that exists in parts of society.

What will this all produce, you ask? A society where justice is served. Far too long have families had to suffer the double injustice of losing a loved one to the streets, while also knowing that the perpetrator roams free, not because the investigation was complex but because no one wants to talk. When this silence is broken, no longer will families have to suffer from this myth.

Add to that, the fact that when dark deeds are readily exposed, the person who committed the crime will actually be punished. It should remind you of the Ecclesiastes 8:11 passage: *when the sentence **is** carried out, people's hearts **are not** filled with schemes to do wrong* (the opposite of the original passage). Our hearts turn to natural justice, the way God made us, because the cover that 'no snitching' seeks to provide the streets is removed. Rather than the gang member becoming more hardened and ruthless because no one wants to comply with the authorities (due to fear and/or pride), he now has to think twice about his actions. Now he recognises how his deeds—that God sees—can easily come into the light. It produces a positive feedback loop, because you know as well as me that when something costs too much, you are unlikely to buy it.

Similarly, when light continuously shines on the activity of the streets, the cost of engaging in dark deeds gets much greater. It deters people—your younger brother, your cousin and even yourself—from gravitating towards or continuing on in the destructive street lifestyle. Funnily enough, rather than people living in fear of being called a snitch, the streets begin to live in fear that someone will actually expose it all. This, in turn, destroys the flawed appearance of trust that exists among the guys in the area, and will mean less darkness and chaos on the streets.

This is what living by God's truth as opposed to this myth can produce. Do you want that? Or do you still fear man rather than God? If it's the former, then remember that you can always trust God. He's got your back!

SCAN TO WATCH THE END OF CHAPTER 4 VIDEO

Alternatively, search www.safehavenprints.com/tsvtk4

WOMEN FOR MY PLEASURE VS. WOMEN, GOD'S IMAGE BEARERS

5

AT FIRST GLANCE, it may seem a bit strange that there is a chapter focusing on women. I mean the streets are usually about young men and, in all honesty, this book is mainly directed at young men like myself that have been poisoned by it.

But that is not to say that women have no involvement or that the streets haven't played a part in tainting our view of them. In fact, during my stint on the streets, I used to hang out with a particular young lady, who was feared and respected by men and women alike. The unfortunate thing is that this respect, in large part, came because she portrayed herself like one of the guys—in appearance, in aggression and character. On the streets, the more like the guys you become, the more you garner respect. That's how the thinking goes. But herein lies the myth that requires dismantling.

So, what's this myth, you ask? Put simply, the myth is that the guys are worthy of respect while women primarily exist for their pleasure. You ever wondered why that dishonourable term usually hurled at women—starting with a 'b'—is used for a gang member that has turned 'soft'? But before we dive in, let me lay out what I believe is the root cause of this myth by giving you an analogy from my school days.

WRONGLY UNDERSTOOD

It may not have been the same for you, but when I was in school, we had various playgrounds for different sports, with the bulk of them set up for playing football. Yet, there was always this playground that had basketball hoops erected. Now, seeing as I'm from England, you would always find more footballs than basketballs at school, so oftentimes you would have people playing basketball with a football—you know what I'm talking about, don't you?

I did it a few times. The grip was never right; the ball would easily slip out of your hands. When it came to dribbling, the bounce back was terrible, and you would have to lower your posture just to keep control of the ball. I think the only benefit from using a football was when it came to shooting. It was much lighter than an actual basketball and your shots glided through the air without using the same force that you would have with a basketball. But apart from that, using a football was horrendous. Not only did it mess up your back, but the game was never as smooth. And, additionally, if you did it long enough, the football would always end up damaged. It would develop an awkward swelling on its side that made it impossible to use again for a proper game of football.

...But it was not this way from the beginning. (Matthew 19:8)

Now why am I telling you all this? Am I taking you down memory lane for no reason? Not at all! If I had asked you to advise my friends and I on how we could have resolved the issues on the basketball court, you probably wouldn't tell me that all we needed to do was replace the football and it would be okay.

No! You'd probably tell us that the football was not made for a game of basketball—this points to purpose—and that I would continue to face these problems as long as I insisted on using a football to play the game. Going a step further, you may have told me that all my issues would vanish if I just bought a proper basketball and played the game as it was intended, the way it was meant to be played from the beginning!

And the exact same reasoning holds true here, when it comes to this chapter's myth: women for my pleasure. The streets train us to mistreat women because it neither understands nor appreciates the reason they were made in the first place. This is the root cause. If only we knew from the beginning the way 'this game' was meant to be played, there would be no myth to demolish. The relationship between men and women is like the basketball game, but the streets approach to this relationship is like choosing to play basketball with a football. Taking this view, it is not a surprise then to find that, on the streets, women are exploited rather than served. When you fail to understand the purpose of a thing, misuse and abuse are to be expected.

Let me give you a few examples!

- *Is it not the case that the ones respected on the streets are also those who have multiple women at their fingertips?*

- *Is it not the case that women's bodies and houses are usually the go-to for storing drugs and weapons?*

- *Is it not the case that loyalty and commitment to one woman is usually scoffed at?*

I wish I could hear your answers to these questions. But if I had been asked to give an answer when I was running around on the streets, it would have been, 'Yes, yes and double yes!' After money—as we looked at in the first two chapters of this book—having women was the next award we all wanted to possess. I surely wanted it and it doesn't seem much has changed.

It was like having the exclusive set of Pokémon cards that everyone collected in primary school, which some still do to this day. If you had them, you were the man. If you did not, then you were like everyone else—average and overlooked. Reading this again, you wouldn't be wrong to question whether I should be comparing a woman to a set of Pokémon cards; but isn't this how women are spoken of and viewed on the streets?

It's as if they're some commodity up for purchase, not for what you can do for them, but solely because of what they can do for you. Think of the Rolex watch in the jewellers, your boys don't crave it for the sake of keeping it clean and pristine. No, they crave the Rolex because of the attention and value it will earn them from wearing it. The Rolex adds to them—not the other way around! Rolex, for my pleasure, you could call it.

Now this makes sense when speaking about a commodity, but not a human being made in the image of God. And, even if you don't appreciate this fact that we are made in the image of God, I know that you would not let anyone think about or approach your little sister, if you have one, in this way. That's why the passage shared earlier—Matthew 19:8 spoken by Jesus—is so fitting in tackling this myth; because from the beginning women were neither intended to be viewed nor treated in this way.

WRONGLY DEPICTED

Have you considered the visuals in music videos? I'm talking your everyday rap video. Apart from the main artist and his friends, some money and a nice car, what else do you tend to see paraded on your screen? Yes, that's right—women, and most definitely wearing something you would not appreciate a female relative of yours wearing online. When you consider that in some instances, you have grown married men—the artist—with multiple women surrounding them in these videos, you have to ask yourself why is it done? No, seriously, why?

Well, when you listen to most of the lyrics that accompany these videos, it's quite clear, isn't it? Most of them say something to the effect of, 'I'm so cool and this is why I have these girls around me, and they do anything I want.' Am I lying when I say that this is the crux of what is communicated? The streets teach that you're powerful if you have 'pretty' women at your disposal. And, to make it worse, you now have female artists—no names mentioned—responding, not with the truth, but with a myth of their own—simply, that men exist for their pleasure.

Now I hope you are seeing how this myth, women for my pleasure, plays itself out and what a distortion it is. I remember being confronted by this reality myself; it wasn't easy. I had to reflect on my time on the streets and how I played with women's hearts solely for my own gain. This was wrong and I am remorseful for it. But, as God started to help me understand why I did this, I started to see that it was rooted in my own personal insecurity of feeling unvalued.

Instead of looking to God, who created me, to understand my worth, I chose, consciously and subconsciously, to adopt this rampant myth on the streets. I believed that if I was *bad* enough, multiple women would like me and that this would accord some type of value to me. It was a lie though, and all it did was destroy relationships and further commoditise women in my eyes.

Maybe you can sympathise with this. I know it's deep stuff, but it is needed because, as I've already shared, when we don't understand the purpose of a thing, misuse and abuse are only around the corner. It is too costly to not understand why woman were made. And you have probably already seen the price some women have paid for this ignorance. When women are viewed solely as objects of pleasure for the guys, there to serve their purposes, it is quite easy to see how on the streets it is okay to commoditise and, in some cases, force a woman to hold drugs and weapons for the gang. If she is nothing but a commodity that you can control, then there will be no concern for her life and well-being because, at the end of the day, the only real concern is your own safety. Besides, she is easily replaceable.

Start children off on the way they should go, and even when they are old they will not turn from it. (Proverbs 22:6)

Now you may say that it is not only women that are targeted for some of these high-risk tasks. And you are right; the streets target anyone that is vulnerable. But in this chapter my focus is on women and the myth that enables them to be viewed as targets. You may also say that this myth—women for my pleasure—did not start on the streets, but is, in fact, a common and widespread notion in society. Again, I would say I am in total agreement with you. However, like that word of wisdom referenced above from Proverbs, when a child is trained in the right way—speaking to values, ethics, role modelling and other such things—as they grow older, it is more likely that they will imitate and adopt what they were taught when young.

So as broader society, especially the media, contributes to the flourishing of this myth, the streets and those who push its false narrative, reinforce rather than counter it. And, for many young teenagers, such as myself when I was that age and possibly you, too, the streets become one of the major places where values are derived. Reflecting on that passage once again then—what do you think becomes of that young man (and the women he engages) who believes that women exist for his pleasure, that his worth is measured by the number of women he dominates and who isn't confronted or changed by the truth? I'll leave that to your imagination.

WOMEN WERE MADE TO REFLECT GOD

So, the obvious question now is: what is this truth? What has God already made known to us that dismantles this myth right at its root? Well, in a short while I'm going to share it. But before I do so, I want to point out something that I observed when I was on the streets. Specifically, it's the way guys related to 'certain' girls as, strangely, these interactions actually reflect the basis of what I want to share.

What is it that I observed on the streets? I'm sure you did also but you may not have linked it to this topic. Well, here it goes. I must confess it was not every girl that was viewed or treated like a commodity on the streets. You probably knew that already. The majority were, but from my observation and personal experience, those ladies who had a brother, relative or some sort of connection to an older that was notorious, were treated very differently.

There was one young lady, Tasha, who I can remember quite well. She had an older brother, Duane, who was well known in the area, and so no one wanted to get on the wrong side of him through mistreating his younger sister. It made sense. The stories about what he had done to people would make you cringe. Therefore, guys, who would normally speak rudely to other girls—with no remorse—knew that they could not try that with Tasha, or else trouble would hit them from all directions.

It follows that they were more ready to take disrespect from her, even though she was a girl, who they could handle if it came to physical combat. This is because Tasha represented her older brother and they could not handle him. You get what I'm talking about, right? We would have never asked her to carry drugs for us and we sure would have thought twice before deciding to cheat on her. She was treated differently—respectfully—by the guys, because of who she represented, or to put it another way, who they revered. The myth didn't really hold with her. Now hold on to that thought.

> *So God created mankind in his own image, in the image of God he created them; male and female he created them.* (Genesis 1:27)

In the Scripture passage above, we get a glimpse into the origin of both man and woman. Put simply, we're told that God created humanity—we're not a product of evolving apes—and that He made both man and woman in His image.

Now this image part may sound complicated, but it should not be. What does an image do? It reflects someone or something. You look in a mirror; you see your image or reflection. And the above passage is saying that God made man and woman in His image, such that when looked at, they are to reflect His character. Now sin, humanity's corruption, has distorted that image, so we fail to reflect God our Creator perfectly. But it does not negate the fact that women were made to reflect and represent God.

THEY HAVE INHERENT VALUE AND WORTH

Now take that in for just one moment! This is the way it was from the beginning—sound familiar? I shared that on the streets there were certain ladies who were fortunate not to undergo the realities of the 'women for my pleasure' myth, due to who they represented. But in this passage, which reminds us of our origins, we see that not some, but *all* women represent One who is greater than the most notorious older you can think of: God Almighty Himself! Let that sink in: every woman represents one that is greater!

Combating this myth therefore involves acknowledging that every woman is God's image bearer. Their worth, identity, value and respect come, not because of anything they have done for you, but because of who they are inherently! I remember when this truth freshly dawned on me, I gradually started to look at women in a completely different light.

In fact, it reminds me of the time I found out I was going to have a daughter as my first child. I was on the bus, and literally every woman I looked at from that moment onwards was a little girl in my eyes, who had a father who loved and cared for her deeply, and would do anything to protect her. They were not a commodity, but a God-crafted human being that was worthy of love. I was going to be that father to my daughter.

And I realised for the first time that she would one day grow up to be one of these young ladies herself. I don't know if you have children, but I'm sure if you did, you would feel the same.

Treat younger men as brothers, older women as mothers, and younger women as sisters, with absolute purity. (1 Timothy 5:1-2)

Now we're imperfect as you can imagine; so too are our daughters. But notice how watchful and caring we are towards them if we have one. How do you think God expects us to be towards those daughters He has made? The very ones in your school, college, Instagram or on TikTok? As you have probably gathered throughout this book, the problem lies within our hearts. This is why in the passage above, God reminds His followers how they are to treat one another. Notice He says that young women are to be treated as sisters—you know, the type of relationship, where you respect, protect, care, and cherish them, without your sister having to do anything for you in return.

Treat the ladies like you would your sister. I know this can sound like a far stretch, especially when you may have spent a good proportion of your life viewing woman through the lens of this myth. I get it. Old habits can die hard. I was once there, and even till this day I intentionally remind myself of God's truth on this matter. The next verse is one I frequently go to. And though it is uniquely aimed at Christian men who are married, it has a lot to say to those men who are not.

Husbands, in the same way be considerate as you live with your wives, and treat them with respect as the weaker partner and as heirs with you of the gracious gift of life, so that nothing will hinder your prayers. (1 Peter 3:7)

So treat all women with consideration, and acknowledge their vulnerabilities, knowing that they are joint heirs with you in the kingdom.

WE PROTECT WHAT WE VALUE

And there's another point to that verse: *so that nothing will hinder your prayers.* Am I right in saying that we protect those things we value? We put locks on our houses and codes on our phones to protect them from intruders. In broader society, we value peace, so we impose fines on those who disturb it. We value life, so we imprison those who take it. You get the gist? So in the passage just cited, do you see what God values and how He goes about protecting it? He values a woman being treated with respect and their husbands giving thought to how they live with them. And what does He do to protect that? He lets her husband know that his prayers *will be hindered* otherwise.

Now you might be thinking what kind of protection is that? Well, to the Christian man, prayer is a lifeline. It is the source of his strength, because prayer ultimately connects him with God. Imagine the drug dealer who loses his plug or has his line confiscated. For him, that is tragic because it is the source of his treasure. The fear of ineffective prayers for a Christian man is like the fear a drug dealer has if his line is taken away; neither wants this to happen.

So by God linking the treatment of one's wife—one valuable thing—to the effectiveness of one's prayer—another valuable thing—God is making real clear to husbands what He values in the marital relationship. Yes, you may not be married; I hear you. But what I hope you take away from this is that, if God desires women to be respected in the first human relationship He chose to establish—a marriage, do you think He would expect anything less from the other types of relationships? Certainly not!

Now I could go further by showing you how, instead of putting women at risk—by making them hold weapons and drugs—to serve your own purposes, Jesus instead shows us that men are called to love their wives as they love themselves (Ephesians 5:25). I could point you to the timeless truth which says, *It is more blessed to give than to receive* (Acts 20:35) and show how this 'women for my pleasure' myth in turn curses us, while portraying itself as a blessing.

But I don't think I have to go there. No, I think the falsehood of this myth is quite clear and that, when you personalise it to the women you hold dear, this saying becomes all the more true for you: *So in everything, do to others what you would have them do to you* (Matthew 7:12). So in closing, my prayer is that God will help you see how valuable women truly are.

SCAN TO WATCH THE END OF CHAPTER 5 VIDEO

Alternatively, search www.safehavenprints.com/tsvtk5

MAKE IT OUT THE HOOD VS. EVIL LEADS TO DESTRUCTION

6

I THINK IT'S SAFE TO SAY that we all love a happy ending. When watching a film, you tell me whether or not you'd feel robbed if something wrong and unfair happened to an innocent character and nothing was done to make things right by the end. You'd probably want to understand the mind of the person who produced such a film, or demand that a Part 2 is released right away. I know I would.

And the simple reason for this is that, as humans made in the image of a Just God, we innately want wrongs to be made right. It is so deep within us. To some extent, that impulse—though misdirected—is the root behind the myth covered in Chapter 3: violence is the way. The obvious point though is that, instead of looking to God (who knows exactly how you feel) for how to respond to being wronged, the streets have riled you up into dealing with it in the heat of your anger. You can appreciate then why a 'happy ending' in such a movie looks more like the perpetrator being repaid for his or her ills, rather than getting away unpunished or even receiving mercy.

But it's not just in films that we're caught looking for a happy ending, is it? Take for example, a person who stops eating sweets, another who trains for a marathon or a young teen who starts saving. Three different people, but I'm sure if they were sat down to explain why they were doing these things, something positive would be at the end of each pursuit. The individual no longer eating sweets may say they're embarking on this in order to avoid catching diabetes, the runner may say they are raising money for a charity helping the homeless, while the teen saving may say they are doing so to set up a business that will serve many.

So, we all look for happy endings, don't we? I'm sure right this minute you can even jot down some personal examples. While it is true, for the most part, that our intents are driven towards obtaining a good outcome from our actions, what if we're hoodwinked? What if we're led into thinking our actions will lead to a happy ending, when in reality, they'll only result in the exact opposite? Has this happened to you before? Well, if not, just know this is the case for those who echo and live by this fifth myth: 'Making it out the Hood'.

ACTIONS & OUTCOMES

Before I get into it, let me give you a sad but familiar example. Have you ever been to the *bookies*[1] before? If you haven't, my hope is that it will remain that way. My wife used to work in one when she was younger and she had stories of some of the distressing things that would happen there. Take Fred, who is a frequent visitor to his local bookies. He's there to make some money that he can hopefully use to treat his family; this is the

---

1   A gambling shop. *See Street Terms for more.*

happy ending he has in mind. Meanwhile, the probability of this actually occurring is slim to none, as most visitors go in with money and come out empty handed. But Fred tells himself that he is different, that it will go well, that he is the lucky one. Minutes go by and now hours, and at this point he has just risked his rent money, as he is confident that this next game will deliver what he came for. I'll stop there because you already know where this ends. But you get the point, right?

Fred is not unique; his hope is that something good will come from his actions. But, tragically, he is deceived, because gambling is no way of trying to treat or provide for your family. In other words, his actions took him down a different road, not the one that would lead to a good outcome. Now you may consider this an extreme example. But can I share something with you? The example I just gave is on par with the deceptive myth that is subconsciously believed and retold on the streets: "I'm only doing this so that I can make it out the hood."

There is a way that appears to be right, but in the end it leads to death. (Proverbs 14:12)

As the above verse makes very clear, though you and I desire great outcomes for ourselves and may know exactly how to attain them, how often do we succeed? There are many times when you embark on a certain course that you deem right or good, only to find out that you are staring death (figuratively speaking) right in the face. Imagine that! Death instead of life! But isn't that a reflection of the streets, what we've been talking about in this book and particularly with this myth!?

FALSE WISDOM

Making it out the hood is the gang member's happy ending, the good outcome he craves. In simple terms, it just means leaving behind the chaos of the ends and being able—at least financially—to relocate or maintain a low profile, without ending up trapped in the system. And, to be honest, it's a desirable objective. I mean, if you haven't arrived there already, there comes a point where you become exhausted with the cycle of violence, the back-and-forth beef, always having to look over your shoulder in case you are caught by an opponent. If you're honest, you must be fed up of the lack of trust and paranoia of getting set up by someone close to you, because a bit of jealousy has crept into the camp.

I remember how my parents shipped me off to Nigeria, to get me away from the life I was leading in London during my teens. Though it was a complete culture shock, it felt like I was being released from a pressure cooker, especially after being chased with a knife only a few weeks before on the streets of London. I was away from the madness of the ends, and though it felt like a punishment at first, I came to realise quite quickly that I did not really want to be living that kind of life anymore. I wanted something better!

You may have walked a similar path or arrived at the same conclusion. But, sadly for many, this is where this myth of making it out the hood starts to take hold. Rather than acknowledging that the streets are a dead end and its worldview should be totally abandoned, the guys on the streets instead tell themselves something to the effect of the following:

'Making it out of the hood is my heaven on earth. And the *only way* I'm going to attain this is by distancing myself from the beef or by delegating it to others to handle for me. This aspect of the streets is negative and a drag on where I'm trying to go. Instead, I'm going to take advantage of the money I can generate through the street network—drugs, fraud, robberies—and make for myself a one-way ticket out of the *hood*, so I don't have to face this anymore.'

Have I missed the mark? Maybe this describes your current thought process or even that of some of the people around you. On the surface it sounds profound, doesn't it? Even wise some will say. But it's not and I'll briefly share how.

Although they claimed to be wise, they became fools... (Romans 1:22)

Before doing so, notice the above passage. I don't want you to miss it. It simply says: *Although they claimed to be wise, they became fools.* In the context, 'they' refers to members of humanity who back in the writer's day—some two thousand years ago—rejected the notion of worshipping the self-existent and all-powerful Creator. Instead, they worshipped images and statues of birds and other animal forms[2]. A quick trip down ancient civilisation lane!

Worship in a nutshell speaks to what we give our ultimate devotion and thanks to in life. With that in mind then, the real contention and impulse behind this passage is that these people rejected God, and gave praise and homage to lifeless objects that resembled inferior creatures. They knew all the while that the beauty and splendour of the universe, the ordering of our

---

2   This is known as idolatry. See *Bible Terms* for more.

seasons, the preciseness and complexity of the human body and much more could never be credited to other gods, let alone animals. Only an awesome and mysterious Creator could be behind it all. Instead of landing here though, they in turn suppressed where the evidence clearly points, and formed alternative theories about the world and our origins. That made them seem wise ... for a little while... though in actuality it made them fools, as their conclusions had real world consequences. Ever heard what happened to animals—cats, in particular—in Ancient Egypt and why? They were buried with their owners when they died, because the people believed they were sacred.

HIDING THE TRUTH

Now how does all this relate to making it out of the hood? Well, put very simply, the thread that joins the two is that in both scenarios the truth was being suppressed. Suppressed you say? Yes! Imagine trying to hold (suppress) a float under water. It will only work for so long, and you may even look wise or strong whilst doing it. But one way or another, it must rise above the surface, and it's in that moment that the fool will be exposed. Reality demands it! Similarly, a society can deny the centrality of an eternal and moral Creator for only so long, before it gradually descends into chaos and starts promoting all types of weird and destructive practices. Already we see this happening in our day; but this is another topic for another time.

Taking it back to Fred at the bookies, gambling is not going to pay the bills. That is the truth and, if you suppress it, it's only a matter of time—thankfully quite quickly—before you feel the pain. It does not matter how nice you dress it; it does not matter who gives a testimonial saying, 'It worked for me;' it just isn't going to cut it. I know I'm preaching to the choir with that one.

But the same is true when it comes to making it out of the hood. It is not wise to try and escape the hood by continuing in the very paths laid out by it. Acknowledging that beef is a drawback, while failing to admit that money made via the streets is also one of the causes of beef, is like trying to use a matchstick to put out a fire. Let it make sense! You might have every good intention, but the end results are going to be devastating.

As I've said before in this book, I swallowed all of these myths at one time or another, so I don't write from a place of pride. I remember trying to build up my money so that I could become more mobile, not quite making it out the hood, but at least so that I could travel outside of my area, avoid beef and not be restricted to my borough. But you could well ask me this question: what do you think you were going to do when you got into other areas? You guessed it: the exact same things I was doing in my very own. You see, the issue was not trying to make it out of the hood, but rather getting the hood out of me. Put another way, the hood—the streets—was too in me for me to escape it. I took it wherever I went. And as long as I suppressed the truth, the happy ending was never going to materialise.

Let me give you another story. There was this particular guy, Jermaine, from my area who was known for fighting. I'm not talking boxing; I mean street beef. This is just what he did and he was good at it. He'd been in and out of jail. And, as you expect, he got older and wasn't on the front line anymore. Years had gone by and I personally had not seen him. But then suddenly I did and we struck up a relationship. In some sense, I was pleased that I had not seen him all that time, as I took it as a good sign that he was keeping out of trouble and staying out the hood the proper way. And, to be honest, that's exactly what he was trying to do.

It wasn't until we started having deeper discussions that I realised that the topic of getting the hood out of his system was the greatest struggle for him. To be honest, I didn't understand the full extent of it. Jermaine didn't want to live the life he was living when he was younger—beef and dumb crime. But he seemed to feel that the only way he could escape the hood was by engaging in higher value—read higher risk—operations outside of the hood. It saddens me to say that we lost contact and the next time I came across him was through a news story that he was back in jail. But sadly, for murder.

INSERT THE TRUTH

A lot more can be said here, such as the mental struggle he was experiencing, and the options that were made available to him to escape the hood the right way. But, as I've had time to reflect on it all, it honestly comes back to this conviction: you're not going to make it out the hood if you suppress the truth about it. Don't follow the myth.

> *For the Lord watches over the way of the righteous, but the way of the wicked leads to destruction.* (Psalm 1:6)

The way of the wicked leads to destruction. Do you know what Fred the gambler in the previous story would have loved? A crystal ball that told him whether the activities he was involved in would get him out of lack, or result in failure. Isn't that the truth? Isn't this what the gambler wants ahead of putting a coin into a slot machine? If he had this foresight, it's likely he wouldn't pursue this path. Then again, the human heart is deceitful as I've shared earlier.

But my point is this: God's Word—the truth—is better than a crystal ball! You don't have to go far to find it, neither do you have to pay to inquire of it. God knows the end from the beginning and therefore His Word is foresight. It lets you and I know the destination before we've even started our journey. You can truly know ahead of time whether you will reach this happy ending by pursuing this myth—making it out of the hood. And the truth, to put it bluntly, is that you will not!

Proverbs 4 urges us to stay away from that path, because it is the way of the wicked:

> *Do not set foot on the path of the wicked*
> *or walk in the way of evildoers.*
> *Avoid it, do not travel on it;*
> *turn from it and go on your way.* (Proverbs 4:14-15)

The beef, the money made illegally, the streets as a whole system and those who follow its course, will end in destruction. This is the truth you need to let sink in and not suppress, if you are still clinging to this myth that the streets have a happy ending. No, the ending is dire and it won't get you to where you want to be. And that is because at the end of evil, at the end of wickedness, lies destruction.

Hear me when I say that God doesn't want this for you.

> Jesus said, *If you hold to my teaching, you are really my disciples. Then you will know the truth, and the truth will set you free.* (John 8:31-32)

Rather than suppressing this truth, you need to believe and allow it to do its work on the inside of you. It's not easy, but it is a much-needed process. I remember when I digested this truth, I made the difficult but worthwhile decision of forsaking the money I had accumulated over the years, and applied for a job at M&S. I knew that making it out the hood through the streets was no longer an option.

Instead, I had to *let go* of the happy ending I thought was possible via the streets, now knowing in light of God's truth that it was a sure path to destruction. I had to look to Jesus and allow Him to guide me to the 'happy ending' that He had in store. It's like a seed that grows into a fruitful tree. You can't expect for it to grow and bear any fruit while you hold on to the seed. But if you *let go* and allow it to be buried in soil, then and only then, can it grow and bear much fruit. Jesus said,

> *Truly, truly, I say to you, unless a grain of wheat falls into the earth and dies, it remains alone; but if it dies, it bears much fruit. Whoever loves his life loses it, and whoever hates his life in this world will keep it for eternal life.* (John 12:24-25 ESV)

My friend, I hope you take it in. More importantly, reject the dreams you've envisioned for yourself on the streets, and embrace what God has. The truth, God's Word, sets us free. While the streets end in destruction, Jesus wants to give you eternal life, which you can experience even now on this earth.

In the closing chapters of this book, we're going to look more closely at Jesus and ultimately how He is the answer to all these myths. In the meantime, let's believe the truth of God rather than the empty memes and sayings of men!

SCAN TO WATCH THE END OF CHAPTER 6 VIDEO

Alternatively, search www.safehavenprints.com/tsvtk6

THE 'REAL' MAN VS. THE TRUE MAN—PART 1

7

YOU'VE MADE IT. We're in the final few chapters, and I want to start with this thought. Everyone wants to be that guy—the real man—the one that everybody looks up to and praises. Don't deny it, deep down inside there is that craving to be respected, to be liked and to be recognised, even by those who don't know you personally. If you are into athletics, I'm sure you've always wanted to be the one who runs the last leg of a 4x100m relay race. And when the baton is handed to you, you lead your team to victory though you started off in third place.

This desire to be great though, isn't unique to you or anyone else who has been caught up with the streets—far from it! This is true of every human being who has walked the earth, except one, and its origin goes back to our first ancestors. Now you may be wondering again, where am I going with all this. Hold on, just wait. Shortly, you will see how this all ties in to this final belief, that in some sense encapsulates every myth we've discussed up to this point. This is a myth that the streets have most likely already posed to you and every individual that has looked its way. Sadly, it continues to serve as a guide for the one who walks down its dangerous path, trying to be the 'real' man.

BACK TO THE BEGINNING

In the book of Genesis in the Bible, we find an account of God creating this earth and every living thing that dwells on it, with humans being the centrepiece of God's great work. In these early chapters, we read about the forming of man and woman, and how they had been given dominion[1] and were created to rule over the whole earth on God's behalf. They (the man, first and foremost) are told that they are free to enjoy and eat from every tree apart from one, and it is at this moment in history where our twisted desire for so-called greatness is birthed. Listen in to this conversation.

> *Now the serpent was more crafty than any of the wild animals the Lord God had made. He said to the woman, "Did God really say, 'You must not eat from any tree in the garden'?" The woman said to the serpent, "We may eat fruit from the trees in the garden, but God did say, 'You must not eat fruit from the tree that is in the middle of the garden, and you must not touch it, or you will die.'" "You will not certainly die," the serpent said to the woman. "For God knows that when you eat from it your eyes will be opened, and you will be like God, knowing good and evil." When the woman saw that the fruit of the tree was good for food and pleasing to the eye, and also desirable for gaining wisdom, she took some and ate it. She also gave some to her husband, who was with her, and he ate it.* (Genesis 3:1-6)

---

1   Power or rulership over nature. See Bible Terms for more.

Now you may be thinking, I would have done the same thing without a shadow of a doubt. If I was given the 'opportunity' to be like God—knowing good and evil—and gain wisdom, I would have snatched it up like there was no tomorrow. And this is exactly what our first ancestors thought and did. Instead of being content with who God created them to be, they desired something different, something else, a new form of humanity as it were, apart from God.

Now in and of themselves, wisdom or greatness are not bad things. That is not what I'm trying to say, nor is this Bible passage alluding to that either. However, when the definition of these two words mean something that's out of step with what God, our loving Creator, has commanded, then problems start to arise. In our ancestors' case, the command to rule over creation, to not eat from a certain tree and ultimately to be relationally dependent on an all-wise God, wasn't wisdom or greatness enough. Instead, being like God, in a way He had not commanded and which they didn't fully understand the consequences of, was something they wanted to aspire to.

Now I'm hoping you are already starting to see how this links to the streets. But if not, if you are still wondering what I am going on about, and how this passage really has anything meaningful to say about the madness on the streets today, then continue reading. To put it another way, ever since our first ancestors believed the lie that they could be great apart from God, going against what He had already defined as right and wrong for them, humans ever since—yes, you and I—have engaged in ever-increasing activities which God calls sinful. We do this in order to fulfil the innate desire to be like God, deciding what is right and wrong for ourselves. All the chapters till now confirm this.

This pattern has led to not only a defacing of what it means to be a true man (as God intended), but an overabundance of poor male role models in our society. These are models of men who make what's right look wrong and what's wrong look right. It is at this point where this passage from the Bible and the myth from the streets of being the 'real' man really meet. Let me press this concept—the abundance of poor male role models—a bit further, so that you can see how this cycle played itself out from the beginning, before showing how it relates to the streets.

THE FIRST KILLER WAS A 'REAL' MAN

The first murderer on record is a man called Cain, our first ancestor's son. And guess who he murdered? His own younger brother, Abel! I can imagine you're reading this and saying to yourself, 'I would never do something like that. I'm not that dumb; neither am I disloyal to my family. Revenge is only for my enemies, and they're definitely not family members.'

But if you're honest, haven't you heard before of two gangs being at war and cousins being a part of either side? I remember during my days on the streets, being in conflict with a group of boys from Deptford, South East London, and a family friend was indeed a part of that very gang. In fact, it saddens me to say that only a couple years ago, I heard about a young man who was killed in South London by a rival gang, and his own cousin was a part of them. You see, the nature of Cain's murder of his own brother is not that unfamiliar with the spirit of the streets today.

Instead of protecting and looking out for his younger brother, instead of learning to offer the kind of sacrifice that was pleasing to God, Cain became jealous of his brother. He invested his energy into murdering him—the very person God had created for him to love and live with. This is an early example of how the idea of what it meant to be a true man steadily shifted. All because his parents sinned (he also followed suit) against their Creator, by choosing to take the sole determination of right and wrong into their hands. I hope you are starting to see how this one act of rebellion not only set things off, but affected all of life in a negative way. Have a read of the account of Cain:

> In the course of time Cain brought some of the fruits of the soil as an offering to the Lord. And Abel also brought an offering—fat portions from some of the firstborn of his flock. The Lord looked with favour on Abel and his offering, but on Cain and his offering he did not look with favour. So Cain was very angry, and his face was downcast. Then the Lord said to Cain, "Why are you angry? Why is your face downcast? If you do what is right, will you not be accepted? But if you do not do what is right, sin is crouching at your door; it desires to have you, but you must rule over it." Now Cain said to his brother Abel, "Let's go out to the field." While they were in the field, Cain attacked his brother Abel and killed him. (Genesis 4:3-8)

So he kills his brother. But, sadly, that's not even the main thing I want you to see. What's even more striking and has a direct link to this myth, is how Cain's descendants responded to this act of violence—the first human murder. I'm not going to quote in full the passage that outlines their response, but you can find it in Genesis 4:23-24. Nevertheless, I will summarise it here for you.

In essence, Cain was praised for his actions. Praised? Yes, praised. In other words, something that should have been condemned is commended; something that doesn't reflect a true man is instead upheld as what it means to be a 'real' man. Does that sound familiar? A sick and deceitful heart? And it is this same ancient and sinful mentality that has found its way into the system of the streets till today.

REFLECT

With all this in mind, why don't you try this thought experiment just for a moment. Seriously, just sit back and think. I'm going to ask you a few questions on topics we have covered to some extent in the other chapters, and I'd like for you to use this time as an opportunity to ponder, rather than give an answer. Ready!?

- *How can it be normal for a young person to aspire to go to jail (in an attempt to earn stripes)?*

- *How can it be standard to learn how to say 'no comment' way before even being arrested?*

- *When did it become attractive to be identified as a murderer/killer?*

- *Why is it so common on the streets to make money from the downfall or addictions of others?*

- *Why is it routine to control and use people for your own selfish gain?*

- *Why is it that we want to become the man who manipulates many women?*

These are just a handful of questions that I think you need to ask yourself and slowly digest. I am in shock as I write this, because these questions outline what my friends and I were striving for until I met the Lord Jesus Christ.

I remember wanting to learn how to box, not in order to engage in the sport or even learn self-defence. I wanted to, so that I could intimidate others and make a name for myself, by knocking out anyone who tried to confront me on the streets (note, this was when fist fights were common!). I even remember daydreaming about how I was going to show off with money—yet to be stolen—from defrauding people of their hard-earned income. This was normal, and sadly, I was not unique in this respect. In a nutshell, these questions summarise and represent the modern gang member, or in other words, what the streets advertise a 'real' man to be. Am I lying?

Is it not true that out of a batch of young people, it is the one who is not afraid to fight, quick to grab a knife and find an enemy that is most feared, most valued and most respected? Was it not the older in the area, who was known for having a quick temper and never allowing any form of disrespect to pass (provided he showed some love to you), that the younger boys looked up to? Isn't this what the streets portray a 'real' man to be?

How about the guy in the area, who because of his illegitimate wealth has different beautiful women at his disposal, with no intention to commit to any of them—is this not what the streets call men to aspire to? Lastly, how about the man who has the car, the nice clothes, the shiniest Rolex, and it is well known that he accumulated this by running a *trap house*[2] managed by young boys, who are risking their lives daily on the frontline. Don't the streets tell you that he is the guy you need to become? It does!

And I've already alluded to the fact elsewhere, that we have a music industry that commercialises and salutes, with no qualms, those who have and still live that life. That is one of the reasons why today you can find some, who have no affiliation with this lifestyle, who know full well that it is ridiculous, but yet do all they can to play the 'real' man of the streets. All they want to do is to take advantage of young people and others like you, who may buy into this culture.

Does this not sound a lot like how Cain's descendants viewed his actions—commendable rather than condemnable? Is this not the streets way of redefining what a true man really is? It is! Same story, different era. And the sad reality is that countless young people like yourself, have and are still falling for this trap. As I've confessed, I was one of them, believing that the streets' image of a 'real' man was something worth becoming. This is the same trap that was set by the serpent—the Devil or Satan—for our first ancestors, when they decided to rebel against God, choosing their own doomed path rather than His life-giving one.

But what if I told you there is a way out? What if I told you that there is One who never fell for this, or any other myth covered so far in this book? That God, yes, the Creator, entered human history by becoming a man, and made His home among us to show us the way. Would you believe it? That God is not only powerful but cares enough to do such a thing for you and I.

---

2   A property from which drugs are produced and sold. *See Street Terms for more.*

THE 'REAL' MAN VS. THE TRUE MAN – PART 1

What if I told you that our Heavenly Father put forward One, who is both the reality and prototype of what a true man really is? That by knowing Him, you would no longer tread the path that has led many to their death, the trap of becoming a "real" man according to the doctrine of the streets. Would you consider this Man, His words and His way? I've introduced Him already, but you're going to see Him, up, close and personal in the chapter that follows.

THE 'REAL' MAN VS. THE TRUE MAN—PART 2

8

THE SYSTEM OF THE STREETS is one of the outcomes of that act of rebellion by the first man Adam, against God. This set into motion the unending cycle of human rebellion, pain and destruction we see in human history. In the verse below, the first part tells us the consequence of sin, but the second part highlights who the solution is.

> *For as in Adam all die, so in Christ all will be made alive.* (1 Corinthians 15:22)

Now, while I've exposed the streets model of a 'real' man, it's time to introduce the true man. What is the difference? In this chapter, I will distinguish the two.

INTRODUCING THE TRUE MAN

The True Man is the One who never once bought into the lie that greatness could be achieved in any way apart from God. Born without sin, He's the One who never fell for the trap, and therefore kept His clothes unstained by sin and rebellion against God. He's the One who confronts the streets depiction of a 'real' man, and gives new life to all who change direction and follow after Him alone. The true man is Jesus Christ.

You may or may not know this, but Jesus is a human in every sense of the word. That's why the Nativity story—till this day—continues to do the rounds at Christmas. It is not a myth; it is real history. He lived on this earth, He had—and still has—a physical body, which bears the marks of the nails in His hands and feet, and the wound on His side where He was pierced. He ate food; He has human relationships. He faced temptation like all of us; yet He did not give into them and sin!

It is this perfect life He models, that sets Him apart from every other man, and therefore why He should be listened to. Though the concept of the streets wasn't a common sight in His day (1st century AD), that myth of being the real man was still alive and well. For example, in Jesus' day, at a time when His country, Israel, was under Roman rule, it was common for a 'real' man to be opposed to Rome and, if it came to it, be willing to violently express his hatred. In fact, this was so normal that other Jews were snubbed—viewed as wastemen—for not defending the cause and siding with the authorities.

Yet, Jesus didn't buy into the politics of the day or the other cultural representations of what a 'real' man should be, despite the pressure to conform to this familiar image. This is one of the most common excuses given by some today as to why they're on the streets. Jesus stands out not only in His era, but in all of human history. Do you know why this is? Why He stood out? It's because Jesus was a man who, first and foremost, was committed to doing God's will. Jesus' identity, and therefore His life, was not rooted in the ever-shifting culture of His neighbourhood, but in the unchanging ways of God. It was God's will or nothing. In other words, He was dedicated to the cause of using His life to fulfil God's plans, no matter the cost. Jesus was a true man because He lived as God originally intended! He is recorded as saying:

> *Then I said, "Here I am—it is written about me in the scroll—I have come to do your will, my God."* (Hebrews 10:7)

You can't deny the extreme contrast here between the motto of Jesus and the motto of the 'real' man of the streets. It's a bit like thunderstorms on one end of an island, and clear blue skies at the other. Our first parents thought it wise to do their own thing rather than God's, and in close succession, their son Cain decided to kill his own brother rather than put on love. In the same way, the streets continue to teach you that pride, respect at any cost and influence, are the height of what it means to be a man.

But Jesus throws all of that on its head with that statement above. It's important you see it, for this is the truth that exposes this myth. This is the truth you need in order to spot what is false. With His life and the words from His lips, Jesus lets us know that a true man is one who acknowledges that his days on earth are to be spent for God. It means doing what He says, and accepting what He determines as right and wrong—rather than taking that role into our own hands (as did our first parents, and you and I).

In that statement, Jesus informs us that a true man is only great when his activities, thoughts, words and self are surrendered to God's will, not to the streets' code of conduct. Moreover, He shows us that a true man values life, and that true life is found only in relationship with God. It is not found in constant rebellion against Him, in contrast to the 'real' man of the streets, whose life eventually leads to eternal death.

That is why Jesus, and He alone, could boldly declare that He is the way, the truth and the *life* (John 14:6). As God in human form (I'll explain shortly), He served the unique role of being the real physical expression of that very life. He makes it clear to all the so-called 'real' men out there, that they can exchange their path of death for His way of life, if they instead look to and trust in Him, the true man.

But that's not all. Jesus continually demolishes this myth of becoming the 'real' man. And I want you to see it, because this false belief is truly the climax of what the streets offer you. This is why I'm spending a bit more time in this final chapter. The more you get to know the person of Jesus, the faster you will want to dismantle that fake concept in your mind, and the sooner you'll want to leave the streets behind and find safety in our Saviour.

THE WAYS OF THE TRUE MAN

In the previous chapter, I gave you some questions to think through (flick back a few pages to recall). These questions may reveal what dominates your current thinking but, will most definitely mirror an active gang member who is still seeking to be the 'real' man. If you asked me to answer why someone would desire such things, despite all the known risks, I would simply put it down to the pursuit of power and influence, and being able to lord it over those who bow to such things—out of fear or deceit. Is this not the truth? Is this not how county lines remain active?

There may be other things at play, for instance, gaining acceptance. But it's no secret that at the heart of becoming the 'real' man of the streets, the hunger for power serves as a driving force for many. I still remember the feeling of pretending to punch an enemy and watching him flinch. It gave me such joy, I didn't want it to end. It made me feel powerful—like I was a 'real' man. Sadly, the same sentiments are echoed loudly today, by some artists, about stabbing people. But let me show you what Jesus has to say about all power play.

> *For even the Son of Man did not come [to the Earth from Heaven] to be served, but to serve, and to give his life as a ransom for many.* (Mark 10:45, emphasis added)

'Son of Man' is a title Jesus used for Himself, but don't let that throw you off. What is Jesus actually saying here? He's making it known that He came into the world to serve people, to lay down His life for the good of others, not to sit back and be served by those under him, like the 'real' man of the streets. Remember the pyramid scheme in Chapter 1?

On one occasion, He took a towel and basin of water and washed the dusty feet of His own followers—a job for servants in ancient Israel. No wonder one of them objected, because he knew Jesus' status as Lord and couldn't understand why He of all people would do such a lowly thing. But Jesus was teaching them by this act that, if He could stoop so low as to wash their feet, they ought to do the same for one another (John 13:1-17). Notice, Jesus stooped low not only in this act, but in first leaving Heaven to come to Earth as an ordinary human, without all His majesty and splendour.

In other words, He demonstrated to His disciples—and to us—that a true man is one who gives and not one who takes when they possess power. Can you picture yourself or the active gang member in your area (who cannot even protect himself in his sleep, let alone run the entire universe), humbling themselves to such a level? Neither can I, because sin, coupled with the worldview of the streets, won't allow you to.

Now you may have just read this statement by Jesus and thought nothing of it. Maybe it sounds motivational to you. I would, too, if I didn't know what I was about to tell you. A man with no power could easily say that he was a servant, but give him an ounce of it, and you will see how quickly he becomes one of the tyrants he once used to condemn. Do you think I'm lying? Have you never seen a young boy who was once timid and quiet, but as soon as the olders recognised and accepted him, his whole demeanour changed? You see, power just exposes what is already present in each of us. But in the case of Jesus—who was and is the true man with all power—He chose to serve, even when the cost of doing so was extremely high! Let me show you how.

Jesus knew that the Father had put all things under his power … (John 13:3)

You see, before Jesus washed His disciples' feet, the author of the above account said He knew that He had immense power over all things. In case you are wondering what 'all things' means, it means all things, nothing excluded—planets, nations, peoples, angels, postcodes, estates—you name it! Jesus is the Boss of Heaven and Earth! Now, in that context, that means the One who holds up the universe, and has the power to bring history to an end, humbled Himself. He cleaned the feet of a few common men, not too dissimilar to you and I.

But that's not all. You may not know this, but in the process of Jesus being wrongfully arrested by the religious leaders of His day, one of His followers struck off their servant's ear, and in response Jesus healed him (Luke 22:47-53). He even warned that a sword was not needed to defend Him, because a multitude of angels would be on-site if He needed them (Matthew 26:51-53). That's right; He had the power to end all His opponents' lives, since He is the One from who they get their breath. But instead, He chose to preserve, serve and love them. Now name me one 'real' man, according to the streets, who would ever do such a thing for his enemies, given the same circumstances—none!

But there is more. Even at His death—one of the most gruesome in human history (Roman crucifixion)—see how He responded to the taunts of His onlookers, 'You saved others ... so why can't you save yourself?' Jesus, the true man, knowing full well that He could, decided to be silent and endure the full weight of suffering: emotionally, physically and spiritually.

THE WORK OF THE TRUE MAN

But why you may ask, was it worth it? Why didn't He just come down from the Cross? I mean, He had His whole life ahead of Him, a young man in His early thirties, with followers and all power. Why this? Well, the answer to this question is what changed my entire life. It exposed the lies and left me despising the streets and its model of a 'real' man. And, instead, it left me craving Him, the Saviour, the true man Jesus Christ. So the answer is simple. In fact, Jesus' own response to this question was that He came into this world 'to serve, and to give His life as a ransom for many.' That's why He didn't come down!

You see, the Bible teaches that you and I were created by a personal God full of deep love for us (Genesis 1:26; John 3:16;

Exodus 34:6), who made us intentionally for His glory. This God is righteous and holy (Psalm 145:17; Isaiah 5:16). It is worth breaking down what righteous and holy mean before moving on. When you hear the words 'holy' or 'righteous', what do you think of? Is it a nun or your eldest relative who attends church services every Sunday? While these reflect popular culture's view of Christian living, in no way do they do justice when defining the righteousness and holiness of God. These attributes of God have to do with His moral perfection (notice, I said perfection), purity and uniqueness. It is not just what He says or does that is good and pure, but it's His very essence and nature as well.

In reference to His holiness, this rhetorical question is usually asked in the Bible: 'Who is like the Lord our God, the One who sits enthroned on high?' (see Psalm 113:5; Exodus 15:11; Psalm 89:6). The answer is no one! He is set apart and there is no one like Him. When it comes to His righteousness or goodness and the things He does and commands, they don't derive their goodness from a customer survey or vote. Or because we hold them up against some common measure of goodness. No, all He does is good and righteous because He is inherently good and righteous!

> ... *God is light, in Him there is no darkness at all.* (1 John 1:5)

All this means that God's nature is the source of true morality in the world, and He expects those He made in His image—us—to reflect this. The above verse perfectly describes Him. Imagine no darkness, meaning evil and sin, no moral imperfection whatsoever. Show me someone who fits that bill!? It's only our Creator who fills such an infinite gap. This is why good and righteous men 'in our eyes' have trembled in the light of God's presence, because in His sight, all their so-called good deeds—that are meant to appease Him—are exposed for what they really are: polluted rags in comparison (Isaiah 6:1-7; Isaiah 64:6)!

Maybe this analogy may help. Imagine, you've had white Nike Air Force 1's for a few years; they're reasonable and you clean them every few weeks. You'd probably think their whiteness was decent, especially after comparing them with friends who had some old pairs as well. But it's only until you get hold of a fresh pair that you'll be convinced that your trainers, despite all the cleaning, continually fall short in comparison to the brand new white pair. In fact, isn't it the sight of the new pair that enables you to see your trainers all the more clearly?!

No competition exists. There are no creases, no bent heels, no stains—these new white pairs are in a league of their own, and any attempt to market your old trainers beside them, would make that billboard an eyesore. Now this is just an analogy, but I hope you're getting the point. The God who made you and I in His image and likeness (Genesis 1:26-27), and to whom we're all accountable, is in a league of His own. He is the height of goodness, love, joy, justice, wisdom, purity—you name it! God is the standard—not a nun, your mother or an angel—and His nature and words give meaning to these terms, because He is perfect (Psalm 18:30)!

Now what does all this mean then? It means that before our holy Creator, each of us is seen for who we truly are. We're human beings, who at the core have rejected Him, chosen our own way and have gone astray in thought, word and deed. No balaclava or facemask can hide you from Him. This is what the Bible calls sin. I hope it's brought to remembrance that ancient lie our first ancestors fell for—to be like God, determining for themselves what is right and wrong. Isaiah, one of the ancient prophets put it this way:

We all, like sheep, have gone astray, each of us has turned to our own way… (Isaiah 53:6)

In truth, I find that most 'real' men on the streets would agree with that statement. They know this deep down. You may even be nodding your head as you read this right now, because your conscience tells you the very same thing. You probably need no convincing that this street lifestyle is sinful in God's sight. I hope you don't. I sure didn't. That is why, for the most part, I tried to hide that life from my parent's sight. And it's why you often find some of these 'real' men abusing substances, so as to suppress the condemning thoughts and flashbacks that frequently prick their consciences.

The truth, however, is that God—our holy and righteous Creator—will not leave guilty lawbreakers unpunished for their sin (Proverbs 11:21). That includes you, me, the nun and every 'real' man according to the streets. You will be judged for how you've lived. None of us are better than the other in God's eyes. Each of us has contributed to what is wicked and wrong in the world, and in God's world we are what those stains and creases are to a fresh pair of white Nike Air Force 1's—all imperfections awaiting judgement.

You may be saying right now, that is harsh. But let me ask you this question: Should the judge of all the Earth not do what is right? Should He allow the thief or murderer of a young man to get away scot-free? Even if the case is closed because witnesses won't snitch? How about the fraudster who defrauds an elderly couple of their hard-earned retirement money? Or the group of men who violently break into your relative's house looking for jewellery?

You already know how our criminal justice system would handle such. In fact, I have a good idea of what you would say or do if this happened to you. So why should we ever think that the Judge of all the Earth, the very definition of justice and fairness, would overlook such things committed in His world? He will do what is right, by punishing those who have done evil on the Day of Judgement (Romans 2:5). He won't overlook any sin, because all these acts and more, at their root, stem from an ultimate rejection of Him who is life! It means you and any 'real' man according to the streets have much bigger problems than the police and lurking opponents. Your biggest concern, should be falling into the hands of the holy and living God upon passing from this life (Hebrews 10:31).

Now I hope you are still with me! I'm sure you're probably thinking how we got here? 'I thought this book was about the streets.' You're right, it is. But as I hope you can now see, the streets and its entire worldview is but a branch of a more deeply rooted issue: human rebellion against God. And at this point you might be asking: 'Is there anything I can do to reverse all this?' You may be saying, 'I know I'm guilty; you don't have to tell me twice. But is there anything I can do to make things right with God?'

It's a good and important question. It's one that I asked myself and others time and time again as I thought about the reality of death. You may have had similar thoughts yourself. But this is why I shared that Air Force 1 analogy because, before God who made us and to whom we're all accountable, all attempts to clean ourselves without Him are ineffective. In the same way that no amount of self-cleaning can restore your old pair to their pristine condition, no amount of giving to the poor, sharing funds with your family or investing in the community—for all the good that they do—can restore you or any 'real' man to a right relationship with our Creator. God says you are dead in your sins (Ephesians 2:1). Take that in for a moment.

It means the solution to your problem lies not in yourself, but in your Creator alone. This solution is what God throughout history, and recorded in the Bible, spent centuries presenting to humanity ever since our first ancestors rebelled. It's the very reason why Jesus, the true man, endured the full weight of suffering on a Roman Cross 2000 years ago, despite possessing all the power to free Himself. It's called salvation! A passage from the New Testament says the following:

> *Here is a trustworthy saying that deserves full acceptance: Christ Jesus came into the world to save sinners—of whom I am the worst.* (1 Timothy 1:15)

What I hope you're seeing is this. The same God who is just, and rightly angry with you and every 'real' man of the streets because of your sin and rebellion, is the same God who out of love for you and every 'real' man of the streets, extends His arm of mercy to save you! When I understood, and believed this, my heart, and subsequently, my life was changed by God.

Throughout the Bible, God makes many promises to a rebellious people—Israel—of rescue from His righteous judgement. He says in Isaiah 1:18, *Though your sins are like scarlet, they shall be as white as snow; though they are red as crimson, they shall be like wool.* God's saying that He's going to make them pure. What a promise! But how was this accomplished in real time, for all people? The passage above makes it crystal clear: it was accomplished through the coming of Jesus!

Jesus didn't always exist as man, but as God, He has always existed. There was a time in history when He entered this world as a baby. He is the Son of God, the One through whom all things were made and who holds all things together (Colossians 1:16-17). It's not 'Mother Nature', 'The Universe', or energy that does this; it's Jesus! Now you may be asking, if Jesus is the Son of God, then who is God?

Put simply, the God who made you and me in His image, has Himself existed from eternity as One Being in Three Persons, who is both personal and relational. God has revealed Himself to various people in history, and those encounters have been recorded and compiled in His Word, called the Bible. It's in the Bible that we come to know that this One God is, in fact, the Father, the Son and the Holy Spirit, three eternal persons, each fully God, who form the One being of God, a term known as the *Trinity*[1].

For God did not send his Son into the world to condemn the world, but to save the world through him... (John 3:17)

And it is this Jesus, that God the Father appointed as the world's Judge (John 5:22), who came into the world to save sinners. Yes, that means you! Have a look at what Jesus said in the passage above. That's right, the Judge of all the Earth came into the world before your court date with Him, in order to make a way to save you from the just condemnation you deserve. Imagine that! Instead of getting rid of the stained and creased

---

1   The unity of God as three Persons as revealed in the Bible. *See Bible Terms for more.*

pair of trainers, He said, 'I will come and make them new.'

Instead of crushing His enemies—all of us who have opposed God in thought, word and deed—Jesus allowed Himself to be crushed willingly for us. Any one of us who turns to Him can now receive His righteous life as a gift. Jesus remained on that Cross not just for the sake of those who taunted Him in the 1st century. Now hear this: He remained there for your sake, you who desires to be the 'real' man of the streets in the 21st century.

Jesus died because the verdict for human sin against God is death, everlasting death (Genesis 2:17; Romans 6:23). And the only escape is for the enemies of God to receive forgiveness, that is, be completely cleansed from sin, declared innocent (now and forever!) and receive a new heart that loves, rather than hates God. This forgiveness could only be obtained if the innocent, holy, perfect, unstained Son of God, Jesus Christ, represented us before God the Father as a human substitute.

> *For our sake he [God the Father] made him [Jesus Christ] to be sin who knew no sin, so that in him we might become the righteousness of God.* (2 Corinthians 5:21, emphasis added)

You could put the above this way—Jesus took what you are, so that you may become what He is! He put on your shirt, by being born as a human not a dog, and lived perfectly in this world before God, in a manner which you haven't come close to achieving for a second. And then, instead of being praised and glorified by God the Father for how righteous He was, Jesus suffered and died on the Cross as if He was a 'real' man according to the streets—as if He had stabbed His opponents from another area, sold drugs from jail, manipulated women into carrying weapons for Him and had many bodies to His name.

That is why from the Cross, Jesus cried out, *My God, my God, why have you forsaken me* (Matthew 27:46)? On the Cross, He took upon Himself, on behalf of sinners, God's righteous judgement against rebellion and sin in His world. Are you taking this in? While Cain's descendants and the streets wrongly commend 'real' men and condemn 'true' men, Jesus Christ graciously chose to be condemned for 'real' men so that they could be commended as 'true' men before His Father.

THE TRUE MAN VS. THE 'REAL' MAN

Take that in for a moment! Can you see the end result of all these myths covered in this book? I hope you do, because their certain end is death and destruction. The wages, or the bag you secure, for your sin against God is death and, without Jesus, you surely will receive it. It is for this reason that Jesus Christ died.

But at the same time, can you see the love and mercy of the true man Jesus Christ? I hope you do. It was due to His love for you that He thought it was worth suffering judgement on your behalf, so that His righteous life could pay for your freedom from the penalty and power of sin. It sounds too good to be true, doesn't it? It's definitely too good, that's for sure, but thank God that this Good News is actually true.

But that's not all. After dying on the Cross in the first century, Jesus Christ, the true man, didn't remain in the grave! Ask around for where His body is, and you'll find that even in His day, people had to make up lies to explain why His body was missing from His tomb only three days later (Matthew 28:11-15)! God raised Jesus from the dead because He was righteous, and it was not possible for Him to be held down by death. He was seen physically by over 500 people; this is proof of Jesus' victory over sin, death and the Devil. When He returns to establish a New Heaven and Earth, Jesus will be the Judge over the living and the dead.

From Heaven, where Jesus sits right now as King, He calls you in this moment to repent and trust in Him. Don't delay; don't think, 'What will my boys say!' This needs to be between you and God. In practical terms, this means confessing your sins to Him, as if you were 'snitching' to the police about all you've done. It means disowning your present life, as if you were forsaking a friend who 'snitched' on you. It means placing your faith in Jesus alone, as you would trust a gun to protect you in enemy territory. Jesus promises that He will never drive away the person who comes to Him (John 6:37). Do this now, and if you're still doubting, read this promise.

> *Therefore he [Jesus Christ] is able to save completely those who come to God through him, because he always lives to intercede for them.* (Hebrews 7:25, emphasis added)

Can you see why Jesus Christ—who died and rose again—will never reject you, just because you come from the streets? Can you see that the streets have offered you a model of a 'real' man that only leads to death, while the true man, Jesus Himself, has come to give you life? Can you see that Jesus dealt not only with this last myth, but ultimately with the biggest myth (and our biggest problem) that has held humanity captive? It's the myth where we tell ourselves we can be like God, and determine for ourselves what is right and wrong. Look at this table for more clarity.

THE 'REAL' MAN VS. THE TRUE MAN - PART 2

THE REAL MAN	THE TRUE MAN
Submits to his plan for his whole life	Submits to God's plan for his whole life
Hates his enemies and seeks to take their life from them	Loves his enemies and lays down his life for them
Follows the streets code of conduct	Follows God's code of conduct
Looks to the streets for his identity	Looks to God for his identity
Lives for his personal/postcodes glory	Lives for God's glory
Seeks to make a name for himself in this temporary life	Has been given a name far above all names both in this life and the one to come
Seeks all power in order to dominate others	Has all power and chooses to serve others
His end is death eternal	His end is life eternal

SCAN TO WATCH THE END OF CHAPTERS 7-8 VIDEO

Alternatively, search www.safehavenprints.com/tsvtk78

CONCLUSION

CONCLUSION

AS I BRING THIS BOOK TO A CLOSE, I hope you've been able to digest all that's been shared, starting with the first myth introduced in Chapter 1, right the way through to the last, being the 'real' man. My hope is that throughout the book you've had moments where you've thought, 'He is hitting the nail on the head—that myth describes me perfectly.' If you have, I take no credit for that, because that is clearly God, through me, reaching out to you. It goes without saying, you can respond to Him directly by speaking what is on your mind—that is the act of prayer [you can also use the Prayer in the next section]. Equally, my desire is that no ounce of confusion remains as to how God and His Kingdom overturns the multiple myths from the streets, through the gift of the true man, Jesus Christ.

If you want to revisit a chapter or even re-read the last one, I'd greatly encourage you to do so. Understanding God's truth is what sets us free, and is the basis for shutting down every other belief the streets have or will ever offer, even those that haven't been covered in this book. It's a foundation that's not easily shaken.

You would appreciate that a lot more pages have been devoted to writing the chapter before this. It was intentional.

And that's because most people only deal with branches when it comes to the streets—the area you're from, for example. God, on the other hand, is in the business of dealing not only with the branches but, first and foremost, with the roots. You can't get rid of a hazardous tree by continually plucking off its branches. At some point, you've got to get to the roots, and that takes time. And to be honest, I cannot say that this book covers everything, but it's a start.

The Bible says Jesus gave Himself for our sins, to rescue us from the present evil age (Galatians 1:4). Though learning a trade, moving to a different area, adopting new friends or earning more income may keep you from the streets, what you ultimately need is rescue from an evil world that you willingly participate in, through your own inclination to sin. The Lord Jesus came to do just that, by bringing us into His Kingdom, to become true men like Himself! He takes us on a journey starting in this life, changing us from the inside out.

And don't I know that to be true. As I've said throughout this book, I wrote this because I know personally how Jesus can completely set one free from the streets and its worldview, and give them life. Don't be deceived by the nice smile at the back of the book or my biography that details some of my achievements to-date. I was a mess. I was lost. And it was in that state, not any other, that Jesus met with me.

I didn't leave school with GCSE qualifications, nor did I finish Year 11 in the same school in which I started Year 7. I got expelled from two schools and ended up in a pupil referral unit (where all the 'bad kids' go) by the time I was fourteen. My deputy head teacher told my mother I would amount to nothing. I had a criminal record before I had even considered what sixth form or college I was going to attend. Based on all the stats, I should have ended up in jail or even worse, six feet under.

Did I have a family? Yes, two parents, though looking back I wish my relationship with my dad had been much better during this period. Side note, the lack of an active father in a young man's life is a major structural issue that needs to be fixed. It's not mentioned as much, but it creates all types of problems that aren't easily resolved. For instance, I craved validation and wanted praise, and I found that I was able to get that in the streets by hanging around certain people, making 'easy' money and playing my part in representing my boys, as and when required. I still remember rolling with a certain older and feeling like I was untouchable. These times, he wanted me to get him some jewellery by robbing others. I was willing to do it, but didn't know who to rob, so I took my mother's jewellery instead. What a mess! But that was my focus, and so I was blind to the train wreck that was waiting to happen.

That's why I got shipped to Nigeria. I thought my parents hated me and couldn't stand me. I now know that wasn't the case. A quick side comment: don't disregard those who tell you hard truths or suggest you make tough decisions. It's such people who usually have your best interest at heart. But, as I said, I didn't agree with my parent's decision. I was no longer on the streets, I was out of sight and I felt isolated. That didn't stop me, however, from continuing my ways in another land.

I ended up getting excluded from my school in Nigeria, because I fought a guy for saying 'Goggle' instead of 'Google'. I look back and laugh now, but that was how petty and willing I was to create a perception of authority and power to those around me. I was insecure. The Streets had taught me well how to mask it, and I had soaked up every lesson. Around the same time, a whole host of my friends were arrested back in London and jailed for a considerable amount of time. I remember hearing the news, and for the first time, I think I actually started to consider where my life was heading.

By the time I was allowed back into school, these questions were still swirling in my head. We were taught about Jesus, and even though I was from a Christian household, I still thought the faith was for older people approaching death or for those who lead boring lives. Certainly not for young people like myself. Add to that, I was very much aware that I wasn't a good person. My teachers in the UK had said this, society thought so and I was in Nigeria for this very reason. So how in the world could God accept me!?

It wasn't until one of the teachers in my school—who also happened to be a Pastor—befriended me and took time to understand my story, that my eyes began to open. It was around this time that the dots started to connect.

Another key point to note, is that speaking through things with trusted people can bring healing. A lot can happen in five years, but for someone active on the streets, those five years have likely comprised violence, near misses, actual deaths, arrests, family pain, fear and many other traumatic events. When on the streets, this feels normal but it really isn't. Unless the realities of these events are brought into the light, the more likely we're going to suffer and live from this brokenness. That's why I value counselling and other pastoral services where this is addressed head on.

But back to this Teacher-Pastor in my Nigerian school. Apart from getting to know me and giving me space to get a lot off my chest, he also shared his past with me. He wasn't caught up in gang culture as I was. But he confessed how before turning to Jesus, he used to dabble in witchcraft in order to manipulate and control people. Wild stuff, I know! I've heard stories of people from the streets using similar tactics to protect themselves from harm. All this to say, that the spiritual world is real and that's why we must trust in the One who made it all, the physical and spiritual.

But the major thing interacting with this teacher showed me, was that God wasn't into rejecting imperfect people, because my teacher definitely wasn't perfect. Jesus put it like this in Mark 2:17:

> *It is not the healthy who need a doctor, but the sick. I have not come to call the righteous, but sinners.*

It was in these moments that my heart and mind started to soften to the person of Jesus and the new life He promised He could give me. But it wasn't until sometime later that I fully decided I'd turn my back on my old life—the streets—and follow Jesus. I wasn't in a church building, nor was I speaking with anyone, but what I can remember is that it felt like a light bulb went on in my head and heart. In that moment, I knew deep down that Jesus loved me and He demonstrated it by dying to take away my sins—all the crimes and mess I had committed on the streets. There was no sin that I had committed that could disqualify me from being a part of His Kingdom. It was then that I became a new creation. I still looked the same, but my desires, outlook and, most importantly, my loyalties started to change.

One example of this was that prior to following Jesus, I couldn't wait to come back to the UK so that I could reunite with my guys and pick up from where I left. But as soon as I put my trust in Jesus, I remember thinking, 'How am I going to come back now? I'm not the same guy I was when I left.' I no longer wanted people to know when I was returning, for fear that I'd get drawn back into the life I'd now left behind. I thank God that He gave me the wisdom and strength to not disclose my return, even to those I was still in contact with.

What really helped during this time were the bonds formed in my church. I met people from all ages, stages and backgrounds, and even one older who used to run with some of the most notorious guys from New Cross, South East London. Being rooted there gave me the much-needed support, friendships, role models and space to grow in my own relationship with Jesus. It wasn't easy, as I had to put off old habits—as I've detailed throughout this book—and an image from the streets that I had embodied for so long. But the joy was knowing God empowering me through it all.

Years later, by now I had completed university, was married and even had a child, I came across a man aggressively handling what seemed to be his girlfriend. She was crying and telling him to stop, and I knew I couldn't just walk by without saying anything. So, as you can imagine, I piped up and said, 'Bro, you need to stop that!' Obviously, he didn't like that I'd intervened and so he came right into my face and started saying all manner of things. What happened next shocked me, because it was only a matter of seconds, but I could hear myself responding to him saying, 'Bro, you don't even know who I am!' But instead of that, I actually said, 'Bro ... God loves you!' Right away he was stunned—me and him actually—and it completely diffused the situation.

I don't know what happened to them after that, but I remember going home that day and honestly thinking, 'I'm a wasteman. How can someone step to me and I respond not with my fist, but with a message of God's love.' God had to remind me that He meant what He said in 2 Corinthians 5:17: *Therefore, if anyone is in Christ, the new creation has come: The old has gone,*

CONCLUSION

the new is here! I no longer reflected the streets, but rather, Christ and His Kingdom. I was changed from the inside out!

I could say much more. But at this point it's not about me and it's all about what God wants to do in you. My story, though special, is not unique, in that this is what Jesus does. He rescues imperfect people, transforms them deep within and sets them on a path of fruitfulness in every aspect—spiritually, relationally, emotionally and socially.

It is my prayer that you turn to Him.

As a next step, why don't you have a look at that table again from the last chapter and ask yourself, 'Do I know any men who pattern their life after the true man Jesus Christ?' It could be a pastor, prison chaplain, parent, youth leader, friend, fellow prisoner, neighbour or a colleague. If you do, then why don't you reach out to them, share what you've taken away from this book and ask them to support you? There's also a high likelihood they'll be a part of a solid church community, so if they haven't invited you already, ask them to bring you along.

And, lastly, if you're reading this and you're a Christian, already following the true man, then why don't you reach out to anyone you know that's seeking to be the 'real' man, and introduce them to Jesus Christ. You don't know, He may work through you to set them free!

PRAYER

HEAVENLY FATHER, I'm thankful that I can speak to you in this moment.

I have lived my life my own way, as my own boss and it has led me down destructive paths.

I've witnessed, experienced and done things on the streets that I know to be wrong (expand on anything specific before God, He already knows). They're not wrong just because society says they are, but because they go against your good law and standard.

Father, I recognise that my greatest problem is sin, and that this has separated me from You. And unless confessed and dealt with, this will separate me from You for all eternity.

Though broken by my past and present, I am thankful that You liken yourself to a Shepherd who goes searching for lost sheep. I've been lost, and I now know that I need You to save me!

Father, I have heard and now believe that You sent your Son, the Lord Jesus, to rescue people like me. That Jesus loved me even while I was active on the streets. And that He died on the Cross to pay the fine for all my sins that I may be forgiven, and rose again on the third day to give me new life and make me right with You.

I ask that you forgive me, and set me free from the lies of the streets. Teach, heal, transform, guide and empower me by Your Spirit to live for Jesus and His Kingdom. Free me from the fear, pride, anger and insecurities that run so deep.

I thank you for this fresh start and that You'll always be with me. And please surround me with those who love and represent You well, so that I too will do the same.

I pray all of this in the Name of Jesus. Amen.

STREET TERMS

BEEF—*conflict that takes place on the streets between different gangs, and sometimes within the same gang. It does not have anything to do with meat in this context.*

BOOKIES—*a gambling shop. If you are not from England, now you know.*

COUNTRY—*a location, usually outside the main city (e.g. London), where drug distribution takes place. Nowadays, it is called 'county lines', but in my era, it was called 'country'.*

ENDS—*the area one is from, which is usually a deprived one. You could refer to South Kensington in London as your 'ends' if you lived there, but it is usually low socioeconomic areas that are referred to as the 'ends'.*

STREET TERMS

OLDER—*an older gang-member, not merely in age, but also in terms of gang hierarchy.*

STREETS—*the gang life and all that comes with it (e.g. the code, people, rivalry, drugs).*

TRAP HOUSE—*a property from which drugs are usually produced and sold.*

WASTEMAN—*someone those on the streets look down on, because, for one reason or another, they don't live up to the streets standard.*

BIBLE TERMS

DOMINION—*rulership over another nation or over nature.*

FORGIVENESS—*means letting go of resentment and giving up any claim to be compensated for the hurt or loss we have suffered. True forgiveness 'keeps no record of wrongs' (1 Corinthians 13:5).*

HOLINESS—*being separate or set apart from that which is sinful. God is holy in that He is set apart from everything that does not conform to His nature.*

IDOLATRY—*the worship of someone or something other than God. The first of the Ten Commandments prohibits idolatry: 'You shall have no other gods before me.'*

RIGHTEOUSNESS—*living in right relationship with God. This means we live justly, honestly, and faithfully according to God's instruction.*

SIN—*the breaking of God's law according to 1 John 3:4. The Greek word it is derived from is 'missing the mark'.*

SPIRITUAL STRONGHOLD—*a false belief that has been fiercely guarded, presenting a great wall of resistance to the Truth. A stronghold could be unreasonable fear, anger or holding on to any of the myths we discussed in this book.*

THE KINGDOM OF GOD—*another term for God's order and reign. It's also a state of living in God's righteousness, peace and joy here on earth because you have accepted Jesus as your Lord and Saviour and follow His way of life.*

TRINITY—*according to the Bible, there is one God, Creator of all things, who exists as three eternal persons, the Father, the Son Jesus Christ and the Holy Spirit.*

CONNECT WITH AUTHOR

Instagram

@Moses.Nw

✉

contact@safehavenprints.com

FOR BOOKINGS AND GENERAL ENQUIRIES